INNOVATIVE APPROACHES TO INDIVIDUAL AND COMMUNITY RESILIENCE

INNOVATIVE APPROACHES TO INDIVIDUAL AND COMMUNITY RESILIENCE

From Theory to Practice

DARLYNE G. NEMETH AND TRACI W. OLIVIER

Neuropsychology Center of Louisiana, LLC.,
Baton Rouge, LA, United States

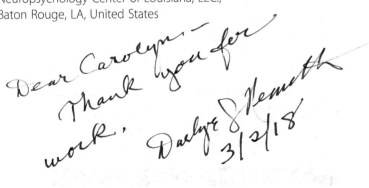

Dear Carolyn –
Thank you for work,
Darlye G Nemeth
3/2/18

ACADEMIC PRESS

An imprint of Elsevier

Academic Press is an imprint of Elsevier
125 London Wall, London EC2Y 5AS, United Kingdom
525 B Street, Suite 1800, San Diego, CA 92101-4495, United States
50 Hampshire Street, 5th Floor, Cambridge, MA 02139, United States
The Boulevard, Langford Lane, Kidlington, Oxford OX5 1GB, United Kingdom

Notices
Knowledge and best practice in this field are constantly changing. As new research and experience broaden
our understanding, changes in research methods, professional practices, or medical treatment may become
necessary.

Practitioners and researchers must always rely on their own experience and knowledge in evaluating and
using any information, methods, compounds, or experiments described herein. In using such information or
methods they should be mindful of their own safety and the safety of others, including parties for whom they
have a professional responsibility.

To the fullest extent of the law, neither the Publisher nor the authors, contributors, or editors, assume any
liability for any injury and/or damage to persons or property as a matter of products liability, negligence or
otherwise, or from any use or operation of any methods, products, instructions, or ideas contained in the
material herein.

British Library Cataloguing-in-Publication Data
A catalogue record for this book is available from the British Library

Library of Congress Cataloging-in-Publication Data
A catalog record for this book is available from the Library of Congress

ISBN: 978-0-12-803851-2

For Information on all Academic Press publications
visit our website at https://www.elsevier.com/books-and-journals

Working together
to grow libraries in
developing countries

www.elsevier.com • www.bookaid.org

Publisher: Nikki Levy
Acquisition Editor: Emily Ekle
Editorial Project Manager: Barbara Makinster
Production Project Manager: Kiruthika Govindaraju
Cover Designer: Miles Hitchen

Typeset by MPS Limited, Chennai, India

CONTENTS

LIST OF FIGURES

LIST OF TABLES

ABOUT THE AUTHORS

Darlyne G. Nemeth, PhD, MP, MPAP, an accomplished clinical, medical, and neuropsychologist, has a broad-spectrum practice at the Neuropsychology Center of Louisiana. Dr. Nemeth was among the first medical psychologists in Louisiana to obtain prescriptive authority. She is a fellow of the American Psychological Association (APA) and served on the APA Council of Representatives for two terms 2010–2016. She served as one of the World Council for Psychotherapy's (WCP) United Nations (UN) Nongovernmental Organization's (NGO) Delegates for 10 years and was Vice President for the US Chapter of WCP for three terms. She is currently serving as WCP's Co-Secretary General.

As an expert in group dynamics, Dr. Nemeth has been nationally and internationally recognized for her Hurricane Anniversary Wellness Workshops, which were offered to the victims/survivors of Hurricanes Katrina and Rita in the summer of 2006. The results of these workshops were presented at the 2013 Meeting of the American Group Psychotherapy Association (AGPA) in New Orleans, LA. Anniversary Wellness Workshop Training Programs were also conducted in China at the 2008 WCP Meeting and in Australia at the 2011 WCP Meeting. In August 2014, Dr. Nemeth gave the Keynote Address on Psychological Leadership in the Event of Environmental Trauma at the WCP Meeting in Durban, South Africa. In 2016, South Louisiana experienced a Great Flood causing thousands to be displaced. Emotional Resiliency Workshops were developed and conducted by Dr. Nemeth, who is also an Environmental Psychologist, to help children, adolescents, and adults cope with this major disaster.

In March 2003, Dr. Nemeth was the lead author on a book titled, *Helping Your Angry Child*, published by New Harbinger. She served as the Lead Editor for the 2012 book, *Living in an Environmentally Traumatized World: Healing Ourselves and Our Planet*, published by ABC-CLIO/Praeger, and the 2015 anthology, *Ecopsychology Advances from the Intersection of Psychology and Environmental Protection*, also published by ABC-CLIO/Praeger. In 2012, Dr. Nemeth was the lead author on an anniversary wellness workshop article that was published in the *International Journal of Group Psychotherapy (IJGP)*. She subsequently published an article in 2013 in *Ecopsychology* on preparing individuals and communities for hurricane anniversary reactions.

Dr. Nemeth served as Director of Neuropsychology at Sage Rehabilitation Hospital Outpatient Services for 5 years. While there, she developed a Hope Therapy Group Program for Brain-Injured Adults, which was presented at the 2013 AGPA meeting in New Orleans. She was also the lead author on an article outlining this process, which was published in *IJGP* in January 2015.

In 2016, Dr. Nemeth was invited to give two keynote addresses at the First Congress on Mental Health: *Meeting the Needs of the XXI Century* in Moscow, Russia: (1) Building Individual and Community Resilience in This Age of Depression and Environmental Trauma and (2) The Influence of Perception on Our Mental Health and Well-being. Subsequently, she has been invited to serve on the Organizing Committee for the Second World Congress on Mental Health in Moscow, Russia in 2018.

Dr. Nemeth obtained a Bachelor's degree from Indiana University in Music and Radio/Television Broadcasting, a Master's degree from Oklahoma State University in Higher Education/Student Personnel, a second Master's degree and a doctoral degree from Louisiana State University in Clinical Psychology, and a Post-Doctoral Master's degree from the California School of Professional Psychology in Clinical Psychopharmacology. Besides being active in the practice of clinical, medical, and neuropsychology and psychopharmacological management, she has written chapters on the history of psychotherapy in the United States, anger management for children, and pediatric medical psychopharmacology.

Dr. Nemeth serves as an externship advisor/mentor for future psychologists. For her outstanding efforts, she was given the 2010 Distinguished Psychologist award by the Louisiana Psychological Association (LPA). Dr. Nemeth serves on LPA's Executive Committee as the APA Disaster Relief Network (DRN) Coordinator for the State of Louisiana. She is also a member of AGPA, where she has obtained recognition as a Certified Group Psychotherapist (CGP), the Louisiana Group Psychotherapy Society (LGPS), and the Louisiana Academy of Medical Psychologists (LAMP). She maintains membership in the International Neuropsychology Society (INS) and the National Academy of Neuropsychology (NAN). Dr. Nemeth has also served as a member and Vice Chair of the Louisiana State Board of Examiners of Psychologists (LSBEP).

Her Web site is www.louisiananeuropsych.com.

Traci W. Olivier, PsyD, earned her doctorate in clinical psychology at Nova Southeastern University in 2016. After completing her internship at the Kennedy Krieger Institute and Johns Hopkins University School of Medicine in pediatric neuropsychology and consultation, she continued her training in pediatric neuropsychology as a postdoctoral clinical and research fellow at St. Jude Children's Research Hospital in Memphis, TN. Throughout her training, she has worked exten-sively with Dr. Darlyne G. Nemeth at the Neuropsychology Center of Louisiana.

Over the course of her graduate career, Dr. Olivier has obtained specialized training in neuropsychological evaluation and intervention with patients across the lifespan, and she has maintained an active role in research over the years. Her particular interests surround pediatric deafness, neurocognitive late effects of cancer-directed treatment, and resiliency in children and adults. She maintains active memberships in professional organizations and regularly presents at conferences such as the APA, the International Neuropsychological Society (INS), the National Academy of Neuropsychology (NAN), and the LPA.

Darlyne G. Nemeth and Traci W. Olivier

PREFACE

The purpose of this book is to define, highlight, and explore the various aspects of resilience in the everyday lives of "ordinary people." It is written by "ordinary people" for "ordinary people." It is not meant to be a scholarly work for scientists, but rather a mainstream anthology for all. It is the intention of the authors to gather pertinent information and life experiences to help us to better understand how resilience affects our everyday lives.

In Chapter 1, Resilience: Defined and Explored, we define and explore the many types of resilience.

In Chapter 2, Resilience: Researched and Evaluated, we evaluate those definitions and attempt to draw an integrated summary of various research findings.

In Chapter 3, Family Resilience: Coping With the Unexpected, we explore healthy as well as unhealthy family dynamics. What children learn or do not learn at home tends to be the basis for how they deal with the world.

In Chapter 4, Community Resilience: Baton Rouge—A Community in Crisis—Grieving and Moving Forward, we focus on a community in crisis and how the process of grieving and moving forward has united its people.

In Chapter 5, Environmental Resilience, we explore how an environment rebounds in the aftermath of trauma.

In Chapter 6, Achieving and Maintaining Individual Resilience, we address how we achieve and maintain resilience, especially when traumas overwhelm our ability to cope.

In Chapter 7, Becoming a Resilient Clinician, we outline the qualities needed to become resilient clinicians and offer an example of one truly remarkable clinician.

In Chapter 8, Promoting Resilience and Fostering Hope, we address the importance of maintaining hope in the face of adversity. We also explore how hope is developed and how resilience can be encouraged.

In Chapter 9, Teaching Resilience, we review the important aspects of resilience that we all must learn if we are to foster resilience in others.

In Chapter 10, Conclusions, we summarize the salient ideas presented in this book and challenge ourselves to embrace our "not so ordinary" future.

It is our intention to offer an understanding of how resilience, hope, connectedness, and commitment propel us to move forward to address the many challenges that lie ahead. Armed with the tools and experiences discussed in these chapters, we are confident that you, the reader, will be better prepared to face them.

Darlyne G. Nemeth and Traci W. Olivier

ACKNOWLEDGMENTS

DARLYNE G. NEMETH, PHD, MP, MPAP

In keeping with our definition of resilience—to be firmly grounded in the present, while learning from the past, so that we can see ourselves in the future—I offer the following acknowledgments and sincere thanks.

The Present

To my wonderful husband, Donald Franklin Nemeth, PhD, geologist, who has been carrying my books since our graduate school days at Louisiana State University (LSU), thank you for making my world beautiful and for introducing me to the importance of cherishing our environment.

To my adventurous brother, Richard Gene Gaynor, MD, internist, who taught me the meaning of living life to the fullest, thank you for always being there for me.

To my elegant sister-in-law, Susanne Maria Jensen, PhD, clinical psychologist, who has been a life-long friend and mentor, thank you for being the epitome of a resilient clinician.

To my amazing research assistants, Jordyn Weydert and Kortney Wooten, without whom this manuscript would not have been possible. Before starting her graduate program in school psychology, Jordyn was instrumental in the development of the first four chapters of this book. Then, Kortney took over and did an amazing job helping us to complete and format this manuscript as did LaJae Coleman who assisted in preparing our final submissions.

To Traci Wimberly Olivier, PsyD, my coauthor on this manuscript, thank you for being the amazing neuropsychologist and woman that you are. I am very glad to have shared this journey with you. I look forward to many wonderful future endeavors.

The Past

To my parents, Marie and Benjamin Gaynor, whose loving relationship guided our family through times of great joy and significant sorrow.

To my husband's parents, Helen and Frank Nemeth, who instilled in Donald the values of loyalty, commitment, and honor.

To my three favorite Washington High School teachers, Edna Stankovich (Home Economics), Dean Croxton (Choir), and Ray J. Krajewski (English), who gave me the tools to succeed at the next level.

To my two most important music teachers at Indiana University—Madame Dorothee Manski, my voice coach, and Dr. George Krueger, my Singing Hoosiers Choir Director—who taught me the joy of musical performance.

To the first psychologist I ever met, Harry Brobst, PhD, at Oklahoma State University, who encouraged me to pursue a doctorate in clinical psychology.

To the three psychology professors at LSU who had the greatest impact on my development as a psychologist:

1. Ralph Mason Dreger, PhD, who introduced me to factor analysis and with whom, I conducted his last, and according to Ralph, his most significant analysis of the six personality types that emerge at times of great change.
2. To Donald Glad, PhD, who introduced me to the value of community psychology.
3. To Virginia Glad, PhD, who introduced me to the field of neuropsychology and the Halstead Reitan Neuropsychological Test Battery.

To my mentors in neuropsychology, Ralph M. Reitan, PhD, and James C. Reed, PhD, who supervised my work in adult and child neuropsychology for many years.

To my two coauthors on *Helping Your Angry Child*, Kelly Paulk Ray, PhD, and Maydel Morin Schexnayder, MS, whose excellent experiences as mothers and professionals enriched our workbook; to Annette McCormick, PhD, LSU associate professor of English, for her editorial comments on this manuscript; and to Monica Schexnayder who brought RILEE Bear to life with her amazing drawing.

To my two coeditors on my subsequent books *Living in and Environmentally Traumatized World*, and *Ecopsychology Advances from the Intersection of Psychology and Environmental Protection* Volumes 1 and 2, Robert Hamilton, PhD, and Judy Kuriansky, PhD, whose insights regarding the science and practice of ecopsychology added depth and breadth to our work. To Bob, whose search for truth and holistic planning regarding the environment is indeed a noble quest, and to Judy, whose dedication to the well-being of all people is so inspiring. I am proud to call you both my colleagues and friends.

The Future

To my intelligent and beautiful daughter, Madeline Nemeth Simmons, of whom I am very proud. To my brilliant son-in-law, David Simmons, who is an excellent husband and father. To my grandson, Colin James Simmons, age 6, who enjoys learning and living life with gusto.

To the many individuals who I have had the privilege to mentor and who are making a difference in their respective communities, thank you for all that you do. This list includes, but is not limited to, the following: Tommy Davis III, Kim Van Geffen, John Robert Hamilton, Julia Hussey, Tiffany Jennings, Traci Wimberly Olivier, Fernando Pastrana, Raphael Salcedo, Chelsie Songy, and L. Taighlor Whittington.

To my current Clinical Assistants, LaJae Coleman and Kortney Wooten, for their dedication and fine work.

To all with whom my paths have crossed, including my dearest friends, Sydney Snyder, Gale Delatte, Bettejean Cramer, Charlotte Gandy, Jean Hamilton, and Peggy Chalaron, your influence is surely present in these pages.

TRACI W. OLIVIER, PSYD

The Present

First and foremost, to the incredibly beautiful and amazing grace I have found through God in Christ. You have taught me, and continue to teach me daily, what it truly means to be resilient. The wisdom I have found through You is the foundation of everything good in my life.

To my dear husband, Lawrence "Law" Olivier, II, MBA. You are one of the most resilient people I know. You have conquered many mountains, yet through everything, you continue to persevere in such a lovely manner. You make everyone around you smile.

To Darlyne G. Nemeth, PhD, MP, MPAP, my incredibly dedicated mentor and friend. What a blessing it was to have met you—truly a divine connection. Words cannot express the gratitude that I have in my heart for everything you have done, and continue to do, for me.

To Marcy Adler, PsyD. You have brought so much light and joy to my life, and you have been there to encourage me through some incredibly dark times. I cannot wait to see what exciting adventures life brings us next.

The Past

To my parents, Thomas "Tim" Wimberly, Jr., and Lorraine Wimberly. Though you are still very much a part of my present, I am forever grateful for your love and guidance. Thank you for always pushing me to do my best and for teaching me the value of education. It has made a world of difference in my life, and I love you.

To Charles Golden, PhD, ABPP. What an honor it was for me to have had the opportunity to work under your guidance. You planted seeds of excellence in my career.

To Jennifer Reesman, PhD, ABPP. Thank you for taking a chance on me. You forever changed the trajectory of my professional life.

To my uncle, Louis Dammerau, for taking the risk with me to redeem the past. You mean the world to me, and I am so grateful that we have such a wonderful relationship in the present.

To all of the friends who have encouraged me along the way, especially during the most difficult times. You are also very much a part of my present, but the love you have given me in the past will not be forgotten. Marcy Adler, PsyD, Sara Schleicher-Dilks, PhD, and Jessica Tsou, PsyD—you made graduate school an unforgettable experience. Together, we made it! To Megan Guerra—you have long been an example and a light in my life. This ship is still going strong! And to all the other numerous friends who have been with me along the way—Annette Potter (the first friend I ever met); Amy Odom Templet, PT, DPT (the first of us to become a doctor! I will never forget your encouragement and the way you used your skills to put me at ease when my father was in the hospital); Mrs. Dory Davis (a true role model in so many ways. You have guided me through many difficult times, and I cherish your friendship); and Beverly Shieh, PsyD (my internship partner; you are such a wonderful friend and a beautiful person).

To Rita Schexnayder, my kindergarten teacher, for planting seeds of faith at such an early age. To Timmy Straight, who taught me to aim for the moon and set high standards, so that even if you fall, you will still be among the stars.

The Future

To my siblings—Thomas Wimberly, III, Triniti Wimberly, and Timi Wimberly. There are so many beautiful days ahead. Be sure to make the most of them. I love you all so very much. And to my beautiful, spunky little niece, Elise Payton—I wish you all the blessings life can offer. You are truly a joy. And to my bright, witty and extremely creative nephews, Caymen and Cruz Tureau. I love you both so very much.

To Kortney Wooten and LaJae Coleman—you have been a tremendous help with regard to this endeavor. Thank you for all of your work and attention to detail, and best wishes for a prosperous and fulfilling career.

To all of those who have poured into my life—it would take another book to properly express my gratitude to you all.

PROLOGUE

When invited to write a book on Resilience by Emily Ekle of Elsevier Publishing, we emphasized the importance of moving past the research and the theories and applying these ideas to everyday life. Most people are resilient. They experience trauma. They falter; but they persevere. It is not that we experience trauma in our lives; it is how we cope with the trauma that we experience that really counts. Coping is a key component of resilience.

The choices that we make are not always good ones. They may work in the short run, but not in the long run. Making wise choices is another very important component of resilience.

When things happen, they are not always "bad." For example, a storm in a drought-stricken area is not always "bad." Torrential rains for days, however, can be devastating. Yet, when we label these events as "bad," we frequently become overwhelmed by our negative thoughts and emotions. These, in turn, propel us to make reactive or unwise choices.

Reactive choices are typically propelled by ideology rather than logic. Most of these choices people live to regret if, like in the aftermath of Hurricane Katrina in 2005, they survived at all.

Planning is another important key to resilience. As approximately 50% of the Earth's people live near water, we must prepare ourselves for environmental disasters. We must have a plan for how we will handle events such as hurricanes, tornados, floods, etc. It is not *if* these weather events will happen, it is *when* they will happen. Most people, however, do not have a plan. When Hurricane Katrina approached New Orleans, LA, many residents partied rather than prepared to evacuate. When they finally realized that evacuation was necessary, it was too late. Interstate 10 North was jammed for hours. It frequently took 8 or more hours just to get to Baton Rouge, a distance of merely 70 miles. This lack of planning led to many unnecessary strandings and deaths.

On the other hand, with Louisiana's Great Flood of 2016, there was no warning. Many seniors in various care centers were awakened with water totally surrounding their beds. Thousands of families from Gonzales to Central, from Baton Rouge to Watson, were flooded out and had to be rescued by boat. As Louisiana is a state where neighbors are used to helping neighbors in distress, the "Cajun Navy" sprang into action. No one called them. They just came. This sense of community is another component of resilience. You just do it, so to speak, because it is the right thing to do. These values of service to one's community are deeply embedded in Louisiana's culture.

Another deeply embedded tradition is that of family. In Louisiana, family matters. Taking care of your parents and grandparents comes first; then you look after yourself. Respect for the elderly is an important component of resilience. We not only learn from the past, but we also respect those who have come before us. For example, in the Great Flood of 2016, one of the most disconcerting issues was the family graves that were unearthed. Due to the water table still being too high, many have not yet been reburied. This grave site desecration has caused considerable angst for many families.

Just like in many Native American communities, the concepts of *respect, reciprocity, responsibility,* and *relationships* are key components of resilience in Louisiana. They are emphasized throughout this book.

Part of our relationship responsibility includes caring for our environment. In the past, Louisianans have not done a very good job of taking care of "Mother Nature." Canals dug through the wetlands by oil companies, for-profit deforestation of the cypress trees along the Gulf Coast, segregated building in low-lying areas, etc., have all contributed to the deadly effects of hurricanes. When these barriers are removed, so are the protections. Protective factors for the land and the people are important components of resilience. When we make short-sighted, for-profit decisions in the short run, we end up paying dearly in the long run. This was one of many factors that made Hurricane Katrina so deadly. For example, the storm surge came right up the human-made "Mr. Go" shipping channel with deadly force. There was no protection. Now, "Mr. Go," which was never fully operational, is defunct and is yet another example of a lack of foresight ending in tragic consequences. Not seeing ourselves in the future, not understanding the importance of holistic thinking, and allowing greed and politics to get in the way have dire consequences.

No matter how resilient people are, they often fall under the weight of such selfish decisions.

Promoting prosocial behavior through community involvement is the essence of resilience. Individuals and communities must function "as one," especially in times of trauma. This is what moving from theory to practice is all about.

Our book focuses on the practical aspects of resilience—how we must be firmly grounded in today, benefit from yesterday, and look forward to tomorrow. We hope that you will enjoy perusing these ideas.

Darlyne G. Nemeth and Traci W. Olivier

CHAPTER 1

Resilience: Defined and Explored

Abstract

The purpose of this chapter is to provide a brief overview of the concept of resilience. Various aspects, perspectives, and definitions of resilience are highlighted and explored. We advocate resilience as a concept that can be learned by "ordinary people." Therefore, on individual and community levels, it is important that we understand how to foster our own resilience in order to teach others how to develop theirs. Within this concept, learning to effectively recognize, label, and share emotions is of the utmost significance. We outline a developmental model of resilience and discuss the implications of attachment theory. We believe that, in today's society, people have become too disconnected, often succumbing to artificial attachments rather than true relationships. Therefore, we perceive connectedness as a key factor in the successful development of resilience, and we believe that individuals must work to maintain and/or reclaim relatedness. Lastly, we discuss the importance of resilience in both the work and home settings.

Keywords: Resilience; perspective; attachment; teaching resilience

Contents

Innovative Approaches to Individual and Community Resilience
DOI: http://dx.doi.org/10.1016/B978-0-12-803851-2.00001-5

The concept of resilience is an ancient one, dating as far back as the 17th century. It stems from the Latin words, "resiliens" or "resiliere," which mean "to rebound, recoil" (Online Etymology Dictionary). Nearly four centuries later, *resilience* has become a mainstream idea, with the use of the word being quite varied and diverse. Current definitions outline resilience as "an ability to recover from or adjust easily to misfortune or change" (Resilience, n.d.). In discussing the "resilient mindset," Goldstein and Brooks (2013) describe such a perspective as allowing individuals "to deal more effectively with stress and pressure, to cope with everyday challenges, to bounce back from disappointments, adversity, and trauma, to develop clear and realistic goals, to solve problems, to relate comfortably with others, and to treat oneself and others with respect" (p. 3).

RESILIENCE CAN BE TAUGHT

Resilience is a trait that can be *taught*. As Spencer points out, "resilience is not a rare ability; in reality, it is found in the average individual and it can be learned and developed by virtually anyone" (2015, p. 27). In his letters to a former SEAL comrade, Eric Greitens constructs the following summary of resilience, its importance, and why it is so difficult for some people to find it:

> Resilience is the key to a well-lived life. If you want to be happy, you need resilience, if you want to be successful, you need resilience. You need resilience because you can't have happiness, success, or anything else worth having without meeting hardship along the way.
>
> To master a skill, to build an enterprise, to pursue any worthy endeavor—simply to live a good life—requires that we confront pain, hardship, and fear. What is the difference between those who are defeated by hardship and those who are sharpened by it? Between those who are broken by pain and those who are made wiser by it?
>
> To move through pain to wisdom, through fear to courage, through suffering to strength, requires resilience.
>
> The benefits of struggling—of being challenged, afraid, pained, confused—are so precious that if they could be bottled, people would pay dearly for them.
>
> But they can't be bottled. And if you want the wisdom, the strength, the clarity, the courage that can come from struggle, the price is clear: you have to endure the struggle first (2015, p. 8).

FOUR TYPES OF PEOPLE

In discussing resilience, we believe that there are four types of people in the world. First, there are those *who have learned how* to be resilient and *actively engage* in the processes and behaviors that foster continued resilience. These are the people who not only survive, but thrive. Second, there are those *who generally know* how to be resilient but have difficulty implementing the behaviors in a practical manner. Therefore, they do not receive the benefit of their knowledge. Third, there are individuals who *know how to become resilient but choose not to* engage in the behaviors and processes that would help them to thrive in life. They choose, in the words of Greitens, not to endure the struggle. Finally, there are those who *simply do not know* how to be resilient.

This book is dedicated to the second and fourth types of people—to those who do not know how to implement resilience in their day-to-day lives, and to those who simply lack an understanding of how to become resilient. Helping people to learn about and develop this meaningful ability is the focus of this book.

MULTIPLE PERSPECTIVES

First, we must understand the many ways in which the word resilience is utilized. With this in mind, perspective, or context, is important. Therefore, the following ideas and definitions are offered to highlight the variety of ways in which resilience has been described by others (in alphabetical order):

- *Community Perspective*: One of the most important community resilience factors is "fostering community cohesion and support" (Berger, 2016, p. 5). Berger continues by explaining that "community cohesion, sense of belonging, as well as trust in the government and local leadership, predicts the probability of developing stress-related symptomatology following exposure to political violence," and that "an important factor... is the community's ability to create a shared meaningful narrative that allows that traumatized community to transform a traumatic experience into a renewal and rebuilding story" (p. 6). Furthermore, as Shaw, McClean, Taylor, Swartout, and Querna note, "The full utility of resilience is often not realized when only conceptualized at the individual level, without attention to its role at the community or system level in trying to promote well-being through research or intervention" (2016, p. 35).
- *Cultural Perspective*: Dr. Panter-Brick describes, "For me, what makes some families more resilient than others is their ability to hang on to a sense of hope that gives meaning and order to suffering in life and

helps to articulate a coherent narrative to link the future to the past and present. That hope or 'meaning-making' is the essence of a cultural perspective on resilience (Panter-Brick & Eggerman, 2012)" (Southwick, Bonanno, Masten, Panter-Brick, & Yehuda, 2014, p. 6).

- *Ecological Perspective*: C.S. Holling, Canadian ecologist, argues that there are two different ways to look at natural systems—as either *stable* or as *resilient*. This perspective implies that resilience is inherently linked to change. Holling refers to the view of systems termed resilience as "a measure of the persistence of systems and of their ability to absorb change and disturbance and still maintain the same relationship between populations or state variables" (Rodin, 2014, p. 48).
- *Economic Perspective*: Rose and Liao (2005) described economic resilience as the "inherent ability and adaptive response that enables firms and regions to avoid maximum potential losses" (p. 76).
- *Emotional Resilience*: Jane McGonigal, game designer, outlined four types of resilience during her 2012 TED talk, one of which was *emotional resilience*. In a blog post, Howe Wallace, Chief Executive Officer of PalletOne, expanded upon the concept of emotional resilience by explaining that individuals who are emotionally resilient "engage in regular reflection on things beautiful, fanciful, visionary" (2015, para. 3). Furthermore, "Emotional resilience exercises our capability to imagine, dream, plan, and create. It fortifies the soul. Emotional resilience allows us to find positive things even when circumstances stay grim" (para. 3).
- *Engineering Perspective*: Youn, Hu, and Wang (2011) describe engineering resilience as "the degree of a passive survival rate (or reliability) plus a proactive survival rate (or restoration). Mathematically, the resilience measure can be defined as the addition of reliability and restoration..." (p. 101011−3).
- *Mental Resilience*: Wallace (2015) describes mental resilience by stating, "You are mentally resilient if you test your brain. Do puzzles. Play board games. Try new hobbies. Read new books. Stay engaged in work. Grow a garden. In short, mentally resilient folks stay challenged" (para. 3).
- *Organizational Perspective*: The resilience of an organization can be defined as the inherent ability to keep or recover the steady state, thereby allowing it to continue normal operations after a disruptive event or in the presence of continuous stress (Sheffi, 2005, as cited in Hosseini, Barker, & Ramirez-Marquez, 2016, p. 48). Others have defined organizational resilience as "the maintenance of positive

adjustment under challenging conditions such that the organization emerges from those conditions strengthened and more resourceful" (Vogus & Sutcliffe, 2007, p. 3418) or "to convey the properties of being *adapted* to the requirements of the environment, or otherwise being able to manage the variability of challenging circumstances the environment throws up" (McDonald, 2010, p. 156). Sheffi further defined resilience for companies as "the company's ability to, and speed at which they can, return to their normal performance level (e.g., inventory, capacity, service rate) [followed by a] disruptive event" (as cited in Hosseini et al., 2016, p. 48). Furthermore, "a resilient organization is a hopeful system because hope is a confidence grounded in a realistic appraisal of the challenges in one's environment and one's capabilities for navigating around them (Groopman, 2004). Hope helps insulate from the vagaries of unexpected events by instilling a belief in the value of constantly updating and refining one's appraisal of the environment and in the organization's ability to use this knowledge effectively in the face of unexpected events" (Vogus & Sutcliffe, 2007, p. 3420).

- *Physical Resilience*: McGonigal (2012) and Wallace (2015) also discussed the physical aspects of resilience. As McGonigal stated, "We know from the research that the number one thing you can do to boost your physical resilience is to not sit still. That's all it takes. Every single second that you are not sitting still, you are actively improving the health of your heart, and your lungs and brains" (13:20). Wallace expanded by stating, "You are physically resilient if you don't sit still longer than an hour at a time. You keep moving, especially when you don't feel like it. I don't know about you, but as I age, the temptation to sit on the couch or to nurse a pain by not moving is high. A physically resilient person works out the kinks and makes physical activity a priority" (para. 3).

- *Physicist's Perspective*: In his 2016 article on traumatology, Berger cites the work of Bodin and Wiman (2004) to describe a resilient substance as "a material that can absorb pressure and bends but bounces back with its original form without being deformed" (p. 4).

- *Psychologist's Perspective*: Spencer states that resilience should be considered a process, rather than a trait one possesses. He describes resilience as a dynamic process whereby individuals exhibit positive behavioral adaptation when they encounter significant adversity, trauma, tragedy, threats, or other significant sources of stress. He refers to resilience as a two-dimensional construct concerning both the exposure of adversity and the positive adjustment outcomes of that adversity, indicating that resilience has been shown to be more than simply the capacity of individuals to cope well under adversity. Resilience may be better understood as the opportunity and capacity of individuals to navigate their way to psychological, social, cultural, and physical resources that may sustain their well-being, and their opportunity and capacity individually and collectively to negotiate for these resources to be provided and experienced in culturally meaningful ways. The American Psychological Association (APA) defines resilience as "the process of adapting well in the face of adversity, trauma, tragedy, threats, or significant sources of stress" (2014, para. 4)[1].

- *Social Perspective*: Adger (2000) defines social resilience as the "the ability of groups or communities to cope with external stresses and disturbances as a result of social, political, and environmental change" (p. 347). Jane McGonigal (2012) lists social resilience as a fourth type of resilience. Wallace (2015) explains, "When you stay in touch with others socially, you are being socially resilient. Hugs and handshakes stimulate the brain. Having a friend who you look forward to visiting with and taking the initiative to stay engaged is social resilience" (para. 3).
- *Structural Perspective*: As Masten states, "We can also constructively think of 'structural resilience'—building robust structures in society that provide people with the wherewithal to make a living, secure housing, access good education and health care, and realize their human potential (Ager, Annan, & Panter-Brick, 2013)" (Southwick et al., 2014 p. 6).

As evident from the above, the concept of resilience has evolved. As Rodin stated, resilience, with its roots in the sciences, is today "a practice, a real-world, hands-on multifaceted process" (2014, p. 53). Perhaps, as Southwick implied, resilience "exists on a continuum that may be present to differing degrees across multiple domains of life" (Pietrzak & Southwick, 2011; Southwick et al., 2014, p. 2) or, as Bonanno (2014) inferred, "Resilience, like trauma, is one of those words that has colloquial meaning" (Southwick et al., 2014, p. 3) and therefore needs to be qualified.

---

[1] Copyright © 2014 American Psychological Association. Reproduced with permission. The official citation that should be used in referencing this material is American Psychological Association (2014). *The road to resilience*. Washington, DC: American Psychological Association. Retrieved from http://www.apa.org/helpcenter/road-resilience.aspx. No further reproduction or distribution is permitted without written permission from the American Psychological Association.

FOUR NEEDED COMMUNITY INTERVENTIONS

When qualifying community resilience, Berger (2016) addresses four important individual/group interventions:

1. Acceptance and expression of feelings in a safe, supportive environment.
2. Awareness of body reactions, as trauma is "essentially a somatic experience" (p. 5) that must be dislodged physically.
3. Enhancement of self-competence by "encouraging people to search for their own abilities and coping skills and to use them" often (p. 5).
4. Promotion of hope and optimism by helping people to "make sense of their experience and to create a narrative that will be meaningful for them" (p. 5).

Berger concludes by defining a resilient society as "The capacity of a community to deal with a major crisis by adapting and growing while minimizing causalities and preserving a fair quality of life for all its citizens and maintaining its core values and identity" (p. 7).

Berger further states that defining resilience as the ability to bounce back is "misguided"; rather, the need is to "incorporate" the experience and move forward. He defines a resilient person as "an individual who has the flexibility and the inner strength to grow from the traumatic event" (p. 7). Furthermore, Berger describes a "resilient community" as one that "has the organizational flexibility and the resources with which they can grow and flourish with time" (p. 7).

ADVERSITY AND ADJUSTMENT

According to Diane Rehm, 90% of individuals will experience some sort of trauma in their lifetime (The Science of Resilience and How It Can Be Learned, 2015). Therefore, people must be prepared to cope with adversity. Using Spencer's definition of psychological resilience, "an individual's ability to properly adapt to stress and adversity," it is important to understand that resilience is a "two-dimensional construct concerning both the **exposure** to adversity and the positive **adjustment** outcomes of that adversity" (2015, p. 27). Thus, the significance of the risk must be considered. For example, in Louisiana, there is a huge difference between a summer afternoon thunder shower and a Category 3 hurricane. Both may be a part of the expected summer weather pattern, but the preparation for and aftermath of these experiences are quite different scenarios.

As Spencer points out, "resilience is better understood as the opportunity and capacity of individuals to navigate their way to psychological, social, cultural and physical resources that may sustain their well-being and their opportunity and capacity individually and collectively to negotiate for these resources to be provided and experienced in culturally meaningful ways" (2015, p. 27). In Louisiana, that capacity completely dissolved in the aftermath of Hurricane Katrina on August 29, 2005.

If, according to Pangallo, Zibarras, Lewis, and Flaxman (2015), "Resilience is a phenomenon that results from the interaction between individuals and their environment (Rutter, 2006) and is not something that individuals initially possess...drawing a distinction between chronic and acute stressors is therefore important" (p. 1). Consistent with the literature, Pangallo and colleagues further identify three components of their "dynamic person-environment definition of resilience as including developmental factors, situational constraints, and sociocultural processes" (p. 2).

ATTACHMENT AND RESILIENCE

In his classic series on attachment and loss, Bowlby (1969) cites secure attachment as one of the fundamentally important developmental processes. It is an instinctual desire for the child to want to attach to the mother and for the mother to desire to offer comfort to the child. In reviewing the work of Ainsworth, Moss, and Yarrow, Bowlby concluded that "how a mother responds plays a leading part in determining the pattern of attachment that ultimately develops" (p. 344). Furthermore, Ainsworth's concepts that contribute to secure attachment are cited as follows: (1) "frequent and sustained physical contact," (2) "a mother's sensitivity," and (3) "a regulated, consistent environment" (p. 345). It is likely that "disturbances of attachment behavior" may undermine a child's ability to develop resilience (p. 357). As Bowlby concludes, "The truth is that the least-studied phase of human development remains the phase during which a child is acquiring all that makes him most distinctively human" (p. 358). Although progress has been made since 1969, there is still much to learn regarding the effects of early attachment security on the development of resilience. Basically, what are the variables that make some individuals more resilient than others?

Situational constraints were observed in the aftermath of Hurricane Katrina. People were separated from their children and pets. Frequently, children were forced to walk in groups, but not with their families, to places where help was allegedly available. Pets, even service dogs, were left behind. Many senior citizens refused to or were unable to evacuate and therefore perished. As cited in the work of Bowlby (1973), "during and after a disaster, people are less reticent" (Baker & Chapman, 1962) and "just being together is deeply important" (Hill & Hansen, 1962). As Bowlby pointed out, being alone "during a disaster is extremely frightening" (1973, p. 167).

ARTIFICIAL ATTACHMENT

Nevertheless, sociocultural processes have created artificial forms of togetherness that appear to undermine this basic need. In her book, *Alone Together: Why We Expect More from Technology and Less from Each Other* (2011), Turkle explores why individuals have a tendency to assign human qualities to objects yet treat other humans as things. She examines the new role of "sociable robots" who "promise a way to sidestep conflicts about intimacy and also express a wish for relationships with limits, a way to be both together and alone" (p. 11).

Is this, according to Turkle, the "new psychology of engagement"? Are robots really going to think for us, feel for us, play with us, and comfort us? How will they promote resilience? Can robots provide alterity? Turkle defines alterity as "the ability to see the world through the eyes of another" and concludes that "without alterity, there can be no empathy" (p. 55). She points out that "children need to be with other people to develop mutuality and empathy" (p. 56). Yet in today's world, children spend more time interacting with screens than they do interacting with people. Now, screens and robots have become babysitters. But what is the price? Are the current generations of children learning to be resilient? Rather, as Turkle concludes, children "are learning a way of feeling connected in which they have permission to think only of themselves" (p. 60). The sociocultural processes that are so vital to resilience are being replaced by technology that is inviting artificial attachment. These various technologies have become "substitutes for the people missing in their lives" and as Turkle states, "will always disappoint because it promises what it cannot deliver. It promises friendship, but can only deliver performances" (p. 101). Turkle concludes that "research portrays Americans as increasingly insecure, isolated, and lonely" (p. 157). Lonely people are not resilient. In their book, *Loneliness: Human Nature and the Need for Social Connection*, Cacioppo and Patrick (2008) conclude that "whatever our own individual sensitivity, our own well-being suffers when our particular need for connection has not been met" (p. 15).

CONNECTEDNESS AND RESILIENCE

When focusing on receptivity and resilience, Cacioppo and Patrick conclude, "When we feel socially connected, as most of us feel most of the time, we tend to attribute success to our own actions and failure to bad luck. When we feel socially isolated and depressed, we tend to reverse the useful illusion and turn even small errors into catastrophes—at least in our own minds" (p. 29).

Cacioppo and Patrick point out that "having the ability to recognize the mental states of others is a capacity called 'theory of mind'" (p. 33). This ability is often challenging for individuals diagnosed with an Autism Spectrum Disorder, which can cause difficulties in social interaction due to trouble perceiving and accurately interpreting social cues. As we substitute interaction with technology for interaction with living beings, both humans and animals, will we be forfeiting this capacity, which is crucial for building resilience?

Emotional regulation, perceptual accuracy, and social disconnection/ disrespect are all capacities that are diminished by loneliness, and loneliness diminishes resilience (Baumeister, Twenge, & Nuss, 2002; Nemeth, 1973). Further evidence is offered by George Williams' book, *Adaption and Natural Selection*, wherein he concludes that "an individual who maximizes his friendships and minimizes his antagonism will have evolutionary advantage, and selection should favor those characters that promote the optimization of personal relationships" (1966, p. 94). Are we optimizing personal relationships by being glued to iPad® screens? Will this increase resilience by promoting adaptation and social cooperation?

Brewer and Gardner (1996) defined a three-part construct of the self—personal, relational, and collective—that requires three categories of social connection: intimate connectedness, relational connectedness, and collective connectedness. All three are required for resilience to flourish. According to Cacioppo and Patrick, loneliness inflicts pain, increases perception of stress, interferes with immune function, and impairs cognitive functioning. They report that the hormone, oxytocin, when released by positive human interaction, can actually intervene to reduce stress reactivity, increase pain tolerance, and reduce distractibility. Could this be our body's organic, physiological contribution to resilience? Perhaps, but it is noteworthy that this release of oxytocin requires human contact. Will this release be negatively impacted by over-involvement with technology? Are our children being raised to be lonely and disconnected? According to Cacioppo and Patrick, "Social isolation deprives us of both our feeling of tribal connection and our sense of purpose" (p. 144). Are the "we" being lost to the technology of the "me"?

RECOGNIZING, LABELING, AND SHARING FEELINGS

Cacioppo and Patrick point out that as people's level of loneliness increases, their ability to accurately interpret facial expressions decreases. In our book, *Helping Your Angry Child* (2003), coauthors Kelly Paulk Ray, Maydel Schexnayder, and Darlyne Nemeth quickly learned that children, even those who would be described as typically developing, had difficulties accurately identifying and interpreting the facial expressions of others. Therefore, an approachable, developmentally appropriate method to teach the facial expression of six important feelings (e.g., angry, happy, scared, sad, embarrassed, and anxious) was used. In the book, the authors did this through the visual representation of a friendly bear named RILEE (i.e., *Relating In Love Every Evening*), using pictures to demonstrate various emotions. Only when the children were able to accurately recognize, label, and share their feelings did the authors proceed to teaching resilient coping strategies. Many of the children in the authors' summer intervention workshops used anger to conceal their loneliness and lack of resilience. Resilience must be carefully taught, but not before the basics of accurate perception of the emotional states of self and others are learned.

Cacioppo and Patrick point out that this process, which we refer to as *empathy*, is derived from the German word *einfühlung*, which is considered to be prelinguistic in nature. Children who have impaired abilities "to discriminate, persevere, and self-regulate," according to Cacioppo and Patrick (p. 191), are prone to lifelong loneliness and, we might add, ineffective resilience. In the final analysis, chronic loneliness increases cognitive dysfunction, paranoia, and social detachment and encourages "parasocial relationships" (i.e., with pets and computers) (p. 256). Is this our destiny?

RECLAIMING RELATEDNESS

Alternatively, as Sherry Turkle (2015) purports, we can *reclaim conversation* if we choose. Turkle indicates that "Online life was associated with a loss of empathy and a diminished capacity for self-reflection" (p. 41). It also reduces resilience. Turkle points out that "average American adults check their phones every six and a half minutes" (p. 42). Adolescents likely check their phones even more often. In referring to the part of our definition of resilience that requires *being grounded in today*, they most certainly are not. According to Turkle, they are not focusing their attention on the present and are therefore missing out on the fullness of interactions and experiences in the present. One only has to remember one's last restaurant experience where many people were likely attending to their cell phones rather than to one another. "We live in a world of unintended consequences," as Turkle points out. "Hyperconnected, we imagine ourselves more efficient but we are deceived". She concluded that, "what is most hopeful is our resiliency", which can be strengthened through conversation (p. 42).

Turkle espouses the value of solitude, rather than constant, 24/7 connectivity. Solitude, however, is not to be confused with loneliness. Solitude is a time, according to Turkle, for reflection, empathy, and perception, which fosters creativity, meta-cognition, perspective, and patience. These are not the values gained by over engagement in social media. Turkle explains that, "instead of promoting authenticity, it encourages performance. Instead of teaching the rewards of vulnerability, it suggests that you put on your best face. And instead of learning how to listen, you learn what goes in an effective broadcast" (p. 109). Social media does not teach or promote resilience. Turkle suggests that "consolation texts" (p. 156) are no substitute for the solace that a face-to-face conversation can provide. Basically, smart phones do not give hugs (at least, not yet!). She cites the essayist, William Deresiewicz, who concludes that our communities have atrophied and that we are now moving from actually being in a community to a *sense* of community, from an actual relationship to a *feeling* of relatedness, from true empathy to a *sense* of empathy, from real relationships to *technological sociable* companions. Perhaps the next step is to regress from *actual* resilience to a *sense* of resilience.

A FALSE SENSE OF RESILIENCE

Many who remained in New Orleans during Hurricane Katrina and its aftermath had a false sense of resilience. It was not real, and it did not last.

Many who stayed perished due to a false sense of resilient security. The following joke was never more true:

A terrible storm came into a town and local officials sent out an emergency warning that the riverbanks would soon overflow and flood the nearby homes. They ordered everyone in the town to evacuate immediately.

A faithful Christian man heard the warning and decided to stay, saying to himself, "I will trust God and if I am in danger, then God will send a divine miracle to save me."

The neighbors came by his house and said to him, "We're leaving and there is room for you in our car, please come with us!" But the man declined. "I have faith that God will save me."

As the man stood on his porch watching the water rise up the steps, a man in a canoe paddled by and called to him, "Hurry and come into my canoe, the waters are rising quickly!" But the man again said, "No thanks, God will save me."

The floodwaters rose higher pouring water into his living room and the man had to retreat to the second floor. A police motorboat came by and saw him at the window. "We will come up and rescue you!" they shouted. But the man refused, waving them off saying, "Use your time to save someone else! I have faith that God will save me!"

The floodwaters rose higher and higher and the man had to climb up to his rooftop.

A helicopter spotted him and dropped a rope ladder. A rescue officer came down the ladder and pleaded with the man, "Grab my hand and I will pull you up!" But the man STILL refused, folding his arms tightly to his body. "No thank you! God will save me!"

Shortly after, the house broke up and the floodwaters swept the man away and he drowned.

When in Heaven, the man stood before God and asked, "I put all of my faith in You. Why didn't You come and save me?"

And God said, "Son, I sent you a warning. I sent you a car. I sent you a canoe. I sent you a motorboat. I sent you a helicopter. What more were you looking for?" (God Will Save Me, n.d.).

Turkle (2015) points out the need to bridge the empathy gap and, in our opinion, the reliance gap. She cites the need to pay full attention to those who are with us in the here and now, to take time to meditate and reflect, and to reclaim the art of conversation. This is what we, as resilient people, must look for and we must recognize it when we find it.

A DEVELOPMENTAL MODEL OF RESILIENCE

A review of the research on depression, youth violence, and resilience by Eisman, Stoddard, Heinze, Caldwell, and Zimmerman (2015) suggested that parent–child communication may help adolescents and their parents maintain close relationships, thereby reducing the negative effects of violence exposure, which are not moderated by sociodemographic factors. Furthermore, for the purpose of their study, Eisman and colleagues adopted the developmental model of resilience defined by Fergus and Zimmerman (2005) as follows: resilience "refers to the process of overcoming the negative effects of risk exposure, coping successfully with traumatic experiences, and avoiding the negative trajectories associated with risk" (p. 399). Eisman and colleagues concluded that applying a resilience framework, identifying the positive factors in adolescents' lives that help them overcome the negative effects of violence exposure, and maintaining parental support "play a vital role in supporting healthy youth development and reducing depression through late adolescence" (p. 1314). As with Turkle, close communication is cited as the key to promoting resilience.

HUMANIZATION AND RESILIENCE

Another important factor is *humanization*. Castro and Zautra (2016) suggest that humanization is "a framework that may guide resilience intervention" (p. 64). For their work, Castro and Zautra offer the 2010 definition of resilience as suggested by Zautra, Arewasikporn, and Davis (2010), which defines "resilient adaptations as a three-dimensional construct, referring to:
a. the speed and thoroughness of stress recovery;
b. the capacity to sustain purpose under stress; and
c. the ability to learn and grow, psychologically from stressful experiences, attaining a greater maturity of mind" (p. 64).

In their study of twin sisters, Castro and Zautra examine the difficulties involved in building and maintaining social relations. Turkle points out how important this skill is, and Castro and Zautra explore the intra- and interpersonal difficulties therein. They suggest that personality and temperament are involved. They point out that a lack of understanding of the importance of maintaining social relations may be at fault. Early life adversity may be a factor, as is, perhaps, a lack of social skills. As Cacioppo and Patrick have described, skewed interpretations of interactions and chronic habit patterns may also be present. Castro and Zautra note that dehumanization may take on many forms. Denying another person's moral sensibility, rationality, individuality, and cognitive depth is one approach. Objectification is another. Ideological beliefs, perceptions of threats, and categorization can also underlie dehumanization. These authors point out the value of Masten's view of resilience as "ordinary rather than extraordinary" (2001, p. 68). Castro and Zautra view resilience "as an outcome—the result of positive adaptation to a stressful experience, while variables that increase the likelihood of these outcomes are defined as resilience resources" (p. 68). Castro and Zautra rely on the work of Folkman and Lazarus (1985), which "argued that emotions serve as adaptive functions in dealing with stress" and suggest "the view of positive emotions as a resilience source has gained considerable empirical support" (p. 69). Castro and Zautra point out that positive emotional experiences can keep depression at bay and can foster resilience. They hypothesize a "Two-Factor Model of Resilience-Encouraging Processes" (p. 69), which includes (1) the Vulnerability (negative) Factor and (2) the Resilience (positive) Factor. These factors can predict the outcomes of social interaction. Furthermore, the latter promotes better sleep hygiene and less loneliness. Castro and Zautra then define the concept of "ego resilience" as a psychological disposition and cite the research of Ong, Bergeman, Bisconti, and Wallace (2006), which demonstrates that greater resilience at baseline was associated with "diminished reactivity to and more rapid recovery from daily stress" (2016, p. 70). Castro and Zautra hypothesize that "social capacities are fundamental ingredients of 'ego resilience'" (p. 70). Castro and Zautra point out that "three decades of social science research has made clear that the relationships we have with one another play a major role in both physical and mental health as we age" and that there is a strong biological link between interpersonal connection and resilience (p. 71). So, then, why do people tend to categorize and/or dehumanize one another? Just because it is easier in the short run does not make it better in the long run.

Castro and Zautra advocate "Social Intelligence Theory," which includes four core principles: (1) Humanization, (2) Uniqueness, (3) Automaticity, and (4) Choice. This training highlights (1) reflective awareness, (2) capacity enhancement for meaningful healing and healthy social connections, and (3) fostering greater resilience when facing challenges and/or adversity (2016, p. 72). Active listening and acknowledging are key; yet, we cannot listen to one another if we are on our cell phones... if we are not fully present.

It is painful to not be heard, to be rejected in favor of the cell phone. Yet this form of social rejection goes on daily. As Eisenberger (2012) points out, social pain is just as "real" as physical pain. In fact, research indicates that "experiences of social pain—the painful feelings associated with social disconnection—rely on some of the same neurobiological substrates that underlie experiences of physical pain" (Eisenberger, 2012, p. 421). Furthermore, Hawkley and Cacioppo (2010) address how chronic loneliness affects our minds. Likewise, social media interactions away from the here and now undoubtedly affect the quality of our relationships. Castro and Zautra describe additional research that emphasizes the decrease in young adults' empathic concerns and perspective in the last three decades and the increase in loneliness among Americans over the last several years. They describe the need for kindness, respect, and social compassion rather than categorization and dehumanization. They conclude by saying "the social, mental, and physical health of each of us advances when we treat one another with humanity" (2016, p. 76). This is an important aspect of resilience.

RESILIENCE IN THE WORKPLACE

We believe this is especially true in the workplace. Crane and Searle (2016) point out that workers, at all levels, face challenges and opportunities for kindness on a daily basis. They hypothesize that challenges can build resilience, which can then lessen the impact of the experience of strain.

But how can resilience be promoted in the workplace and elsewhere? Spencer (2015) outlines 11 factors that can help in this regard. They are as follows:

1. "The ability to cope with stress effectively and in a healthy manner.
2. Having good problem-solving skills.
3. Seeking help.
4. Holding the belief that there is something one can do to manage your feelings and cope.
5. Having social support.
6. Being concerned with others, such as family or friends.
7. Self-disclosure of the trauma to loved ones.
8. Spirituality.
9. Having an identity as a survivor as opposed to a victim.
10. Helping others.
11. Finding positive meaning in the trauma" (p. 29).

Furthermore, Spencer includes 10 ways to build resilience as suggested by the APA (2010). They are as follows:

1. "To maintain good relationships with close family members, friends and others;
2. to avoid seeing crises or stressful events as unbearable problems;
3. to accept circumstances that cannot be changed;
4. to develop realistic goals and move towards them;
5. to take decisive actions in adverse situations;
6. to look for opportunities of self-discovery after a struggle with loss;
7. to develop self-confidence;
8. to keep a long-term perspective and consider the stressful event in a broader context;
9. to maintain a hopeful outlook, expecting good things and visualizing what is wished; and
10. to take care of one's mind and body, exercising regularly, paying attention to one's own needs and feelings" (p. 30).

RESILIENCE FOR THE HOMEPLACE

But not all people can benefit from these ideas. Holmes et al. (2015) examine resilience in physically abused children. Frequently, aggression is their only outlet. Protective factors are key to helping children develop the resilience to "overcome significant risks or adverse experiences and achieve positive developmental outcomes" (p. 177). They define resilience as "the capacity for successful adaptation in the face of adversity" and point out that "resilience is a dynamic developmental process." They define protective factors as "prosocial skills, child internalizing well-being, and caregiver well-being" (p. 178). Prosocial skills are further defined as including self-control, cooperation, assertion, and well-being. Internalizing well-being is defined as "the absence of internalizing behavior problems," and a caregiver's well-being includes "the absence of maternal drug dependence, few symptoms of mental health problems, and few maternal depressive symptoms" (p. 179). Their results suggest that physically abused children were more likely to exhibit aggressive behavior than children who were not physically abused. Obviously, physical abuse is a severe form of dehumanization and, in the authors' opinions, likely decrease one's ability to develop resilience. Holmes and her colleagues further conclude that "a child's individual characteristics are more strongly related to resilience and positive functioning in the face of maltreatment, compared with his or her interpersonal relationships and environment" (p. 184). They also note that "successful early adaptation increases the probability of continued successful adjustments in later life" and that caregiver-level protective factors have "windows of opportunity" to influence this outcome by helping maltreated children to develop resilience and lessen their reliance on aggression (p. 185).

TEACHING RESILIENCE RATHER THAN AGGRESSION

Americans are experiencing increasing levels of aggression as a result of categorization, dehumanization, and terrorism. Resilient coping skills appear to be diminishing. Whatever the cause, the importance of teaching resilience, rather than aggression, is now becoming an urgent matter.

Judith Rodin, in her 2014 book, *The Resilience Divide*, begins to address this problem by defining five characteristics of resilience:

1. Aware → As knowing one's strengths and assets
2. Adaptive → As having the capacities to adjust to changing circumstances
3. Diverse → As having multiple capacity to adjust to changing circumstances
4. Integrated → As being able to coordinate one's functions (feelings) and actions when needed
5. Self-Regulating → As being able to deal with difficult situations and disruptions without extreme malfunction or catastrophic collapse.

She further states that we must be ready, responsive, and vitalized to build resilience. Rodin concludes that resilience is a never-ending process that provides a number of benefits, many of which are not always obvious. Resilience, however, should not be confused with change; rather, it is about absorbing and adapting. Resilience is not about achieving permanent stability, but rather about absorbing disruption without collapse. It is adaptive. Rodin reminds us that "resilience is a concept, with roots in the sciences, that has today evolved into a practice, a real-world, hands-on, multifaceted process of resilience building that we can all learn and master" (p. 53). She points out that three factors make community resilience so essential—urbanization, climate change, and globalization. In this regard, Rodin cites Kate Lydon, who states that "the fundamental insight is preparedness; which, along with resilience, are about human connections" (p. 165).

THOUGHTS OF RESILIENCE, CULTURE, AND STRUCTURE

Leading experts in the field of resilience participated in a plenary panel at the 2013 meeting of the International Society for Traumatic Stress

Studies. They included Steven M. Southwick, George A. Bonanno, Ann S. Masten, Catherine Panter-Brick, and Rachel Yehuda. Their thoughts on *Resilience Definitions, Theory, and Challenges* (2013) are summarized in the following section.

DEVELOPING DEFINITIONS OF RESILIENCE

- *Steven Southwick*: "Resilience more likely exists on a continuum that may be present to different degrees across multiple domains of life (Pietrzak & Southwick, 2011)" (p. 2).
- *George Bonanno*: "Resilience as a stable trajectory of healthy functioning after an adverse event" (p. 2).
- *Rachel Yehuda*: Resilience may co-occur with Posttraumatic Stress Disorder. Moving forward in an insightful and integrated positive manner, "as a result of lessons learned from an adverse experience" (p. 3).
- *Ann Masten*: Resilience is "the capacity of a dynamic system to adapt successfully to disturbances that threaten the viability, the function, or the development of that system (Masten, 2014a, 2014b)" (pp. 3—4).
- *Catherine Panter-Brick*: Resilience as a process to harness resources to sustain well-being (Panter-Brick & Lechman, 2013)" (p. 4).

Cultural resilience, according to Panter-Brick, states that "what makes some families more resilient than others is their ability to hang on to a sense of hope that gives meaning and order to suffering in life and helps to articulate a coherent narrative to link the future to the past and present. That hope or 'meaning-making' is the essence of a cultural perspective on resilience (Panter-Brick & Eggerman, 2012)" (Southwick et al., 2014, p. 6).

Structural Resilience, according to Ager et al. (2013), is defined as "building robust structures in society that provide people with the wherewithal to make a living, secure housing access, good education, and health care, and realize their human potential" (p. 6).

The panel then outlined the following childhood protective factors that have routinely been identified in developing resilience:

1. A healthy attachment relationship and good caregiving
2. Emotional regulation skills
3. Self-awareness and the capacity to visualize the future
4. A mastery motivation system that drives the individual to learn, grow, and adapt to their environment.

They concluded that being able to use flexible coping strategies to address the specific challenges or traumatic events at hand, to adjust these strategies accordingly, and to alter their use as the situation further develops is the embodiment of true resilience. They also commented that resilience-enhancing interventions "can be administered before, during, or after stressful/traumatic situations," but that preparative training is best (p. 12).

We believe that the hallmark of resilient people is their ability to be firmly grounded in today, to benefit from yesterday, and to imagine themselves in tomorrow. In order to develop resilience, one must mindfully and actively engage in the following coping strategies, as offered by Nemeth and Whittington (2012). First, it is important that individuals learn how to effectively recognize and face their feelings and share their experiences with others. Second, individuals must learn to acknowledge and affirm both their own feelings and experiences as well as those of others. Only after completion of the first two steps can people begin the third step—identifying and solving problems. Next, individuals must engage in a process of ongoing reassessment and reprioritization of needs to avoid repeating unhelpful aspects and/or mistakes of the past. Lastly, individuals must implement the things they have learned from the previous four steps. This is arguably the most important step, as knowledge without intervention is useless.

Therefore, throughout this book, we will offer preparative training coping strategies that "ordinary people" can use to foster resilience in their lives and in the lives of their families and communities.

REFERENCES

Adger, W. N. (2000). Social and ecological resilience: Are they related? *Progress in Human Geography, 24*(3), 347–364.

Ager, A., Annan, J., & Panter-Brick, C. (2013). Resilience—From conceptualization to effective intervention. *Policy Brief for Humanitarian and Development Agencies.* Retrieved from http://jackson.yale.edu/sites/default/files/documents/Resilience_Policy Brief_Ager Annan Panter-Brick_Final.pdf.

American Psychological Association. (2014). *The road to resilience.* Washington, DC: American Psychological Association. < http://www.apa.org/helpcenter/road-resilience.aspx >.

Baumeister, R. F., Twenge, J. M., & Nuss, C. K. (2002). Effects of social exclusion on cognitive processes: Anticipated aloneness reduces intelligent thought. *Journal of Personality and Social Psychology, 83*(4), 817.

Berger, R. (2016). An ecological-systemic approach to resilience: A view from the trenches. *Traumatology: An International Journal.* http://dx.doi.org.ezproxylocal.library.nova.edu/10.1037/trm0000074.

Bodin, P., & Wiman, B. (2004). Resilience and other stability concepts in ecology: Notes on their origin, validity, and usefulness. *ESS Bulletin, 2*(2), 33–43. Retrieved from https://www.researchgate.net/publication/236208772_Resilience_and_Other_Stability_Concepts_in_Ecology_Notes_on_their_Origin_Validity_and_Usefulness.

Bowlby, J. (1969). *Attachment and loss* (Vol. 1), New York: Basic Books.

Bowlby, J. (1973). *Separation: Anxiety and anger* (Vol. II, Attachment and Loss), New York: Basic Books.

Brewer, M. B., & Gardner, W. (1996). Who is this "we"? levels of collective identity and self representations. *Journal of Personality and Social Psychology, 71*(1), 83−93. http://dx. doi.org.ezproxylocal.library.nova.edu/10.1037/0022-3514.71.1.83.

Castro, S. A., & Zautra, A. J. (2016). Humanization of social relations: Nourishing health and resilience through greater humanity. *Journal of Theoretical and Philosophical Psychology, 36*(2), 64−80. http://dx.doi.org.ezproxylocal.library.nova.edu/10.1037/ teo0000040.

Cacioppo, J. T., & Patrick, W. (2008). *Loneliness: Human nature and the need for social connection.* New York: W.W. Norton & Company, Inc.

Crane, M. F., & Searle, B. J. (2016). Building resilience through exposure to stressors: The effects of 2013 challenges versus hindrances. *Journal of Occupational Health Psychology, 21*(4), 468−479. Available from http://dx.doi.org/10.1037/a0040064.

Eisenberger, N. I. (2012). The pain of social disconnection: Examining the shared neural underpinnings of physical and social pain. *Nature Reviews Neuroscience, 13*(6), 421−434.

Eisman, A. B., Stoddard, S. A., Heinze, J., Caldwell, C. H., & Zimmerman, M. A. (2015). Depressive symptoms, social support and violence exposure among urban youth: A longitudinal study of resilience. *Developmental Psychology, 51*(9), 1307−1316. Available from http://dx.doi.org/10.1037/a0039501.

Fergus, S., & Zimmerman, M. A. (2005). Adolescent resilience: A framework for understanding healthy development in the face of risk. *Annual Review of Public Health, 26,* 399−419.

Folkman, S., & Lazarus, R. S. (1985). If it changes it must be a process: Study of emotion and coping during three stages of a college examination. *Journal of Personality and Social Psychology, 48*(1), 150−170. http://dx.doi.org.ezproxylocal.library.nova.edu/ 10.1037/0022-3514.48.1.150.

God Will Save Me. (n.d.). Retrieved July 18, 2016 from http://epistle.us/inspiration/ godwillsaveme.html

Goldstein, S., & Brooks, R. B. (2013). Why study resilience? In S. Goldstein, & R. B. Brooks (Eds.), *Handbook of resilience in children* (2nd ed.) (pp. 3−14). New York: Springer. Available from http://dx.doi.org/10.1007/978-1-4614-3661-4.

Greitens, E. (2015). *Resilience: Hard-won wisdom for living a better life.* New York: Houghton Mifflin Harcourt Publishing Company.

Groopman, J. E. (2004). *The anatomy of hope: How people prevail in the face of illness.* New York: Random House.

Hawkley, L. C., & Cacioppo, J. T. (2010). Loneliness matters: A theoretical and empirical review of consequences and mechanisms. *Annals of Behavioral Medicine, 40*(2), 218−227.

Holmes, M. R., Yoon, S., Voith, L. A., Kobulsky, J. M., & Steigerwald, S. (2015). Resilience in physically abused children: Protective factors for aggression. *Behavioral Sciences, 5*(2), 176−189.

Hosseini, S., Barker, K., & Ramirez-Marquez, J. E. (2016). A review of definitions and measures of system resilience. *Reliability Engineering and System Safety, 145,* 47−61. Retrieved from http://www.sciencedirect.com.ezproxylocal.library.nova.edu/science? _ob = ArticleListURL&_method = list&_ArticleListID = -1022710560&_sort = r&_st = 13&view = c&md5 = c2b20e5523a4cb9bfae017bcc7539563&searchtype = a.

McDonald, N. (2010). Organisational resilience and industrial risk. In D. D. Woods, & N. Leverson (Eds.), *Resilience engineering: Concepts and precepts* (pp. 155−179). Vermont: Ashgate Publishing Company.

McGonigal, J. (2012). *Jane McGonigal: The game that can give you 10 extra years of life* [Video file]. Retrieved from https://www.ted.com/talks/jane_mcgonigal_the_game_that_can_give_you_10_extra_years_of_life

Nemeth, D. G. (1973). *The efficacy of laboratory training as a method of retarding or reversing the disengagement process among senior citizens* (Unpublished doctoral dissertation). Louisiana State University, Baton Rouge, LA.

Nemeth, D. G., Ray, K. P., & Schexnayder, M. M. (2003). *Helping your angry child: Worksheets, fun puzzles, and engaging games to help you communicate better.* Oakland, CA: New Harbinger Publications, Inc.

Nemeth, D. G., & Whittington, L. T. (2012). Our robust people. In D. Nemeth, R. Hamilton, & J. Kuriansky (Eds.), *Living in an environmentally traumatized world: Healing ourselves and our planet* (pp. 113–140). Santa Barbara, CA: Praeger.

Ong, A. D., Bergeman, C. S., Bisconti, T. L., & Wallace, K. A. (2006). Psychological resilience, positive emotions, and successful adaptation to stress in later life. *Journal of Personality and Social Psychology, 91*(4), 730.

Pangallo, A., Zibarras, L., Lewis, R., & Flaxman, P. (2015). Resilience through the lens of interactionism: A systematic review. *Psychological Assessment, 27*(1), 1–20. http://dx.doi.org.ezproxylocal.library.nova.edu/10.1037/pas0000024.

Panter-Brick, C., & Eggerman, M. (2012). Understanding culture, resilience, and mental health: The production of hope. In M. Ungar (Ed.), *The social ecology of resilience: A handbook of theory and practice* (pp. 369–386). New York: Springer.

Resilience. (n.d.). *Online Etymology Dictionary.* Retrieved July 11, 2016, from http://www.etymonline.com/index.php?term = resilience

Resilience [Def. 2]. (n.d.). *Merriam-Webster Online.* Retrieved July 14, 2016, from http://www.merriam-webster.com/dictionary/resilience

Rodin, J. (2014). *Being strong in a world where things go wrong: The resilience dividend.* New York, NY: Public Affairs.

Rose, A., & Liao, S. Y. (2005). Modeling regional economic resilience to disasters: A computable general equilibrium analysis of water service disruptions. *Journal of Regional Science, 45*(1), 75–112.

Shaw, J., McLean, K. C., Taylor, B., Swartout, K., & Querna, K. (2016). Beyond resilience: Why we need to look at systems too. *Psychology of Violence, 6*(1), 34–41. Retrieved from http://search.proquest.com.ezproxylocal.library.nova.edu/docview/1756074242?accountid = 6579.

Shaw, J., McLean, K. C., Taylor, B., Swartout, K., & Querna, K. (2016). Beyond resilience: Why we need to look at systems too. *Psychology of Violence, 6*(1), 34–41. Retrieved from http://search.proquest.com.ezproxylocal.library.nova.edu/docview/1756074242?accountid = 6579.

Southwick, S., Bonanno, G., Masten, A., Panter-Brick, C., & Yehuda, R. (2014). Resilience definitions, theory, and challenges: Interdisciplinary perspectives. *European Journal of Psychotraumatology, 5.* http://dx.doi.org/10.3402/ejpt.v5.25338.

Spencer, L. (2015). Psychological resilience. *Mid Yorks Medical Journal, Summer, 2015,* 27–30. Retrieved from https://issuu.com/midyorksmesh/docs/my_medical_journal_summer_2015?e = 0/30055614.

The Science of Resilience and How It Can Be Learned [Audio blog interview]. (2015). Retrieved July 18, 2016, from http://thedianerehmshow.org/shows/2015-08-24/the-science-of-resilience-and-how-it-can-be-learned.

Turkle, S. (2015). *Reclaiming conversation: The power of talk in a digital age.* New York: Penguin Press.

Turkle, S. (2011). *Alone together: Why we expect more from technology and less from each other.* New York: Basic Books Publishing.

Vogus, T. J., & Sutcliffe, K. M. (2007). Organizational resilience: Towards a theory and research agenda. In *2007 IEEE international conference on systems, man and cybernetics* (pp. 3418–3422). IEEE.

Wallace, H. (2015). The four types of resilience [Web blog post]. Retrieved from https://www.palletone.com/ceo-blog/the-four-types-of-resilience/

Williams, G. (1966). *Adaptation and natural selection: A critique of some current evolutionary thought.* New Jersey: Princeton University Press.

Youn, B. D., Hu, C., & Wang, P. (2011). Resilience-driven system design of complex engineered systems. *Journal of Mechanical Design, 133*(10), 101011.

Zautra, A. J., Arewasikporn, A., & Davis, M. C. (2010). Resilience: Promoting well-being through recovery, sustainability, and growth. *Research in Human Development, 7,* 221–238. Available from http://dx.doi.org/10.1080/15427609.2010.504431.

CHAPTER 2

Resilience: Researched and Evaluated

Abstract

This chapter explores current research on resilience, beginning with the four waves of resilience as outlined by Ann Masten. The following includes, but is not limited to, a review of a number of measures designed to evaluate resilience. The authors discuss factors and systems involved in adaptivity, discussing its relevance to resilience. They also describe the effects that childhood experiences have upon one's ability to develop resilience. Nevertheless, they posit that resilience can be learned. Lastly, discussions of the Katrina 10 Wellness Workshops and future directions for research (including the relevance of Situational Judgment Tests) are provided.

Keywords: Measurement; adaptivity; childhood experience; wellness workshops

Contents

Dr. Ann Masten, in her 2014 book titled *Ordinary Magic: Resilience in Development*, and in previous works (Wright, Masten, & Narayan, 2013), outlined four major waves of resilience science, which are as follows:

- *Wave 1—Descriptive: Identification of individual resilience and contributing factors.* In this wave the focus is on *what* questions, specifically questions that help us to define, measure, and describe resilience.
- *Wave 2—Process: Including resilience in broader systems (e.g., developmental, ecological).* In this wave the focus is on *how* questions—specifically, how do we protect, promote, and prevent people from developing pre- and/or post-trauma symptoms?
- *Wave 3—Interventions: Fostering resilience.* The focus is on *when* it is necessary to promote resilience.

Innovative Approaches to Individual and Community Resilience
DOI: http://dx.doi.org/10.1016/B978-0-12-803851-2.00002-7

- *Wave 4—Integration of Technology and Knowledge: Incorporating research on resilience in systems and processes (e.g., epigenetics, neurobiological).* Here, the focus is on *why* questions—why can genetics, statistics, and neuroscience bring about more dynamic and systems-oriented approaches to resilience?

We understand the above waves to focus on (1) What matters, (2) How the process of resilience works, (3) When can interventions be helpful, and (4) Why new approaches can improve resilience methods. Questions about *who* and *where* also need to be asked—specifically, who can benefit from resilience training and where can this training best be offered?

The focus of this chapter is to explore the current research questionnaires that allow us to better understand *who* is or is not resilient, and *how* and *where* resilience can be further developed in people.

RESILIENCE AND ADAPTIVITY

According to Masten (2014), intact neurocognitive functions, competent close relationships, effective schools and communities, opportunities to succeed, and healthy beliefs nurtured by a positive world are salient factors in promoting resilience. Would not it be wonderful if such a world existed? But ours is merely a world in progress. In the meantime, Masten defined resilience as referring to the "capacity (potential or manifested) of a dynamic system to adapt successfully to disturbances that threaten system function, viability, or development; positive adaptation or development in the context of significant adversity exposure" (p. 308). This is the world in which the majority of us live. Therefore, adaptation is crucial. Without adaptation, people do not survive and thrive. For individuals, Masten reports that resilience requires exposure to adversity and coping in its aftermath. Furthermore, she offers the following table of "short list" common resilience factors (adapted from Masten, 2014, p. 148) (Table 2.1).

Risk factors may include negative experiences, whereas, assets may include special talents or resources. Masten (2014) hypothesizes "that child cognitive skills and parenting quality would play a protective function in children faced with adversity" (p. 71). On the idea of a "positive manifold," Masten writes, "Competent people tended to have more positive self-concepts and higher self-esteem, a variety of positive personality traits. . .and better social understanding, attention regulation, planning, and creative thinking" (Masten et al., 1999, 2004; Pellegrini, Masten,

Table 2.1 Masten's short list resilience factors

Resilience factors	Adaptive systems
Effective caregiving and parenting quality	Attachment; family
Close relationships with other capable adults	Attachment; social networks
Close friends and romantic partners	Attachment; peer and family systems
Intelligence and problem-solving skills	Learning and thinking systems of the central nervous system (CNS)
Self-control; emotion regulation; planfulness	Self-regulation systems of the CNS
Motivation to succeed	Mastery motivation and related reward systems
Self-efficacy	Mastery motivation
Faith, hope, belief life has meaning	Spiritual and cultural belief
Effective schools	Education systems
Effective neighbors; collective efficacy	Communities

Garmezy, & Ferrarese, 1987; Shaffer, Coffino, Boelcke-Stennes, & Masten, 2007). Competent people also had more external resources and social capital in the form of adult support inside and outside the family (e.g., Masten et al., 1988, 1999, 2004) (p. 74). Thus, competent and resilient individuals have similar adaptive advantages. Whereas, their maladaptive counterparts reacted more to stress, became upset more easily, and were, in general, less conscientious and agreeable.

COMPETENCE CAN BE LEARNED

Masten's position is that "competence begets competence" (p. 73). Our position is that competence can be taught/learned, which in turn, promotes and fosters the advancement of competence. Even though resilience can be learned, as Masten points out, self-control is critical. As Southwick and Charney describe, "individuals who are temporarily (or, in some cases, permanently) unable to think clearly or regulate their words will have difficulty" learning resilience strategies (2012, p. 20). Oftentimes, people lose control and give way to aggression because they do not know how to recognize, label, and share their feelings in healthy ways. Being able to do so begets healthy relationships.

THE EFFECTS OF CHILDHOOD EXPERIENCES

Childhood poverty undermines positive development and adaptation. Feeling loved, safe, and securely bonded to a mother figure are crucial for children to survive and thrive, to be resilient. Thus, according to Masten (2014), negative emotionality, stress reactivity, and ruminating on negative experiences can exacerbate a traumatic shock even further. The loss or separation from significant caregivers can also undermine a child's well-being. In the event of a disaster, therefore, communities must reform quickly and work effectively to restore the basic survival and safety needs of their children.

Masten (2014) reminds us that resilience in young people depends on their individual attributes, the context of their experiences, and the quality of their relationships. As described by Bowlby (1982), Masten reiterates the importance of attachment. Furthermore, she identifies self-regulation skills such as "self-management of attention, arousal, emotions, and actions, [that] also appear to play a central role in human adaptation, development, and resilience" (p. 156). Other important attributes include "hope, optimism, faith, and [the] belief that life has meaning" (p. 164). An agreeable temperament, humor, self-confidence, emotional stability, and conscientiousness are also protective effects for resilience (Masten, 2014).

HOW CAN THESE QUALITIES BE MEASURED?

Wouldn't it be nice if such qualities could be measured? In an effort to learn more about this, we set out to review the literature to search for resilience questionnaires. We subsequently came across the following article titled *Resilience Through the Lens of Interactionism: A Systematic Review* by Pangallo, Zibarras, Lewis, and Flaxman that appeared in the 2015 edition of the *Psychological Assessment* journal published by the American Psychological Association (APA). The authors identified 17 resilience measures published since 2013 and noted many "inconsistences associated with the definition and operationalism of resilience" (p. 1). They explored Rutter's (2006) definition of resilience, which is "a phenomenon that results from the interaction between individuals and their environment and not something that individuals innately possess" (p. 1). Further into their article, the authors relied on Windle's (2011) conceptualization of a working definition of resilience, which is "the process of effectively negotiating, adapting to, or managing significant sources of stress or trauma. Assets and resources within the individual, their life and environment facilitate this capacity for adaptation and 'bouncing back' in the face of adversity. Across the life course, the experience of resilience will vary" (p. 152). From Windle's definition the authors outlined the following three conceptual components: "a) the presence of significant stress that caries substantial threat of a negative outcome (antecedent), b) individual *and* environmental *resources* that facilitate *positive* adaptation and c) positive adaptation or adjustment relative to developmental life stage (consequence)" (Pangallo et al., 2015, p. 2). The authors then iterated that they adopted the following definition of resilience, "that resilience culminates from an individual's interaction with [his/her] environment which, in turn, is influenced by developmental factors, situational constraints, sociocultural processes (Luthar, Cicchetti, & Becker, 2000; Vanderbilt-Adriance & Shaw, 2008)" (p. 2). They concluded that resilience is a dynamic person/ environment phenomenon, explaining the importance of a person's trait resilience and "the need for measures capable of predicted variations in resilient outcomes" (p. 2).

The authors suggested that, as Funder (2009) stated, "A new direction that has been prominently suggested for the future of personality psychology is to alter the traditional focus on between-person variance to yield a sharper view of within-person variance" (p. 122). In addition, they suggested that, perhaps, the focus needs to be on dynamic interactionism (i.e., "how individuals and situations mutually influence one another" [p. 2]). They then offered a review of the advantages and disadvantages of the following 17 self-report measures:

1. Baruth Protective Factors Inventory (BPFI; Baruth & Carroll, 2002)
2. Connor-Davidson Resilience Scale (CD-RISC; Connor & Davidson, 2003)
3. 10-item Connor-Davidson Resilience Scale (CD-RISC-10; Campbell-Sills & Stein, 2007)
4. Abbreviated Connor-Davidson Resilience Scale (CD-RISC2; Vaishnavi, Connor, & Davidson, 2007)
5. Multidimensional Trauma Recovery and Resiliency Scale (MTRR; Harvey et al., 2003)
6. Abridged Multidimensional Trauma Recovery and Resiliency Instrument (MTRR-99; Liang, Tummala-Narra, Bradley, & Harvey, 2007)
7. Resilience in Midlife Scale (RIM; Ryan & Caltabiano, 2009)
8. Resilience Scale for Adults (RSA; Friborg, Hjemdal, Rosenvinge, & Martinussen, 2003)
9. Trauma Resilience Scale (TRS; Madsen & Abell, 2010)

10. Resilience Scale (Wagnild & Young, 1993)
11. Ego Resiliency-89 (ER; Block & Kremen, 1996)
12. Revised Ego-Resiliency 89 Scale (ER-89-R; Alessandri, Vecchione, Caprara, & Letzring, 2012)
13. Personal Views Survey III-R (PVS-III-R; Maddi et al., 2006)
14. Psychological Capital Questionnaire (PCQ; Luthans, Youssef, & Avolio, 2007)
15. Sense of Coherence Scale (SOC; Antonovsky, 1993)
16. Brief Resilient Coping Scale (Sinclair & Wallston, 2004)
17. Brief Resilience Scale (BRS; Smith et al., 2008)

As presented in Table 2.2, Pangallo et al. (2015, p. 1029) suggested that the following higher-order resilience themes and subthemes, derived from these various scales, were important.

Southwick and Charney (2012) also reviewed several measures in their book: *Resilience: The Science of Mastering Life's Greatest Challenges*, which included the following:

1. Connor Davidson Resilience Scale (CD-RISC; Connor & Davidson, 2003)
2. The Response to Stressful Experiences Scale (RSES; Johnson et al., 2008)
3. The Dispositional Resilience Scale-15, which includes the following three dimensions: being fully engaged; having a sense of control over events, and being able to view adversity as a challenge (Bartone, 2007)

Table 2.2 Pangallo et al.'s higher-order resilience themes and subthemes

	Themes	Subthemes
Internal resources	Adaptability	Flexibility
		Acceptance openness
	Self-efficacy	Positive self-esteem
	Affective coping	Acceptance
	Positive emotions	Optimism
		Hope
	Mastery	Internal locus of control
		Resourcefulness
	Hardiness	Commitment
		Control
		Challenge
External resources	Supportive relationships	Social competence
		Family coherence
	Structured environment	Planning
		Organizing
	Conceptual adequacy (parent scales)	

4. The Resiliency Scaled for Children and Adolescents, which includes the following three dimensions: mastery, relatedness, and emotional reactivity (Prince-Embury, 2008).

Additionally, Southwick and Charney (2012) defined 10 "resilience factors," which include "realistic optimism, facing fear, moral compass, religion and spirituality, social support, resilient role models, physical fitness, brain fitness, cognitive and emotional flexibility and meaning and purpose" (p. 13).

THE KATRINA 10 WELLNESS WORKSHOPS

With this in mind, the authors chose to include a measure of resilience (the CD-RISC by Connor & Davidson, 2003) in their Katrina 10 Wellness Workshops. This was one of the four instruments that Pangallo et al. defined as having "demonstrated acceptable psychometric properties" and moved beyond "the measurement of person variables to define resilience" (2015, p. 17). The authors noted that CD-RISC included items relating to external support, which was an important factor in the Katrina 10 Wellness Workshops, which were offered to New Orleanians who suffered from Hurricane Katrina on August 29, 2005. Efforts were made to provide wellness workshops one year post-trauma and again 10 years post-trauma to assist participants with resilient coping. These workshops were sponsored by the Louisiana Psychological Association and cosponsored by the APA, the Louisiana Group Psychotherapy Society, the World Council for Psychotherapy, the Recovery Center of Baton Rouge, and the Baton Rouge Area Society of Psychologists and were offered free of charge to the public. In the 2006 workshops, no measure of resilience was utilized; however, in the 2015 workshops, the workshop leaders requested and were granted permission from Connor and Davidson to use their CD-RISC, which measured the following themes through Likert scale ratings: adaptivity, relatedness, spirituality, stress, confidence, humor, coping, resilience, comfort, effort, goals, hope, support, focus, initiative, grit, strength, decisiveness, emotion, impulsivity, purpose, control, discovery, effort, and pride.

FUTURE DIRECTIONS

In the meantime, the authors, along with Fernando Pastrana, PhD, clinical and neuropsychologist, are endeavoring to develop their own measure of resilience with Hurricane Katrina in mind. Because it was not fully developed by the time of the 2015 workshops, however, the CD-RISC was the measure of choice to address resilience.

Pangallo et al. also suggested the need for a Situational Judgement Test (SJT) approach and cited the work of Motowildo and Beier (2010). They further noted the research of House, Kahn, McLeod, and Williams (1985) that identified the need for three distinctive dimensions that should be included: "(a) emotional (understanding, empathy and concern), (b) instrumental (concrete actions that networks may perform such as physical assistance, financial assistance, or practical assistance) and (c) informational (guidance or advice)" (p. 16).

Perhaps SJTs could be helpful in training individuals to develop resilience. For many years, the Johari Window Test (Luft & Ingham, 1961), a type of SJT, has been used to facilitate group process intervention and increase awareness. Other tests, such as Hall and Williams' forced-choice Personnel Relationship Survey (1987), rely on understanding participants' behavior in interpersonal relationships through the lens of the Johari Window. Such concepts and SJTs may prove to be useful resiliency education strategies.

REFERENCES

Alessandri, G., Vecchione, M., Caprara, G., & Letzring, T. D. (2012). The Ego Resiliency Scale revised. *European Journal of Psychological Assessment*, *28*, 139−146. Available from http://dx.doi.org/10.1027/1015-5759/a000102.

Antonovsky, A. (1993). The structure and properties of the sense of coherence scale. *Social Science and Medicine*, *36*, 725−733. http://dx.doi.org/10.1016/0277-9536(93) 90033-Z.

Bartone, P. T. (2007). Test-retest reliability of the Dispositional Resilience Scale-15, a brief hardiness scale. *Psychological Reports*, *101*(1), 943−944.

Baruth, J., & Carroll, K. (2002). A formal assessment of resilience: The Baruth Protective Factors Inventory. *The Journal of Individual Psychology*, *58*, 235−244.

Block, J., & Kremen, A. (1996). IQ and ego-resiliency: Conceptual and empirical connections and separateness. *Journal of Personality and Social Psychology*, *70*, 349−361. Available from http://dx.doi.org/10.1037/0022-3514.70.2.349.

Bowlby, J. (1982). *Attachment and loss*. New York: Basic Books (Original work published 1969).

Campbell-Sills, L., & Stein, M. B. (2007). Psychometric analysis and refinement of the Connor-Davidson Resilience Scale (CD-RISC): Validation of a 10-item measure of resilience. *Journal of Traumatic Stress*, *20*, 1019−1028. Available from http://dx.doi.org/10.1002/jts.20271.

Connor, K. M., & Davidson, J. R. T. (2003). Development of a new resilience scale: The Connor-Davidson Resilience Scale (CD-RISC). *Depression and Anxiety*, *18*, 76−82. Available from http://dx.doi.org/10.1002/da.10113.

Friborg, O., Hjemdal, O., Rosenvinge, J. H., & Martinussen, M. (2003). A new rating scale for adult resilience: What are the central protective resources behind healthy adjustment? *International Journal of Methods in Psychiatric Research*, *12*, 65−76. Available from http://dx.doi.org/10.1002/mpr.143.

Funder, D. C. (2009). Persons, behaviors and situations: An agenda for personality psychology in the postwar era. *Journal of Research in Personality, 43*(2), 120−126. Available from http://dx.doi.org.ezproxylocal.library.nova.edu/10.1016/j.jrp.2008.12.041.

Hall, J., & Williams, M. S. (1987). Personnel relations survey. *Teleometrics International.*

Harvey, M. R., Liang, B., Harney, P. A., Koenen, K., Tummala-Narra, P., & Lebowitz, L. (2003). A multidimensional approach to the assessment of trauma impact, recovery and resiliency. *Journal of Aggression, Maltreatment & Trauma, 6*, 87−109. Available from http://dx.doi.org/10.1300/J146v06n02_05.

House, J. S., Kahn, R. L., McLeod, J. D., & Williams, D. (1985). Measures and concepts of social support. In S. Syme, & S. Leonard (Eds.), *Social support and health* (pp. 83−108). San Diego, CA: Academic Press.

Johnson, D. C., Polusny, J. A., Erbes, C., King, D., King, L., Litz, B., et al. (2008). The Response to Stressful Experiences Scale (RSES). *Military Medicine, 176*(2), 161−169.

Liang, B., Tummala-Narra, P., Bradley, R., & Harvey, M. R. (2007). The Multidimensional Trauma Recovery and Resiliency Instrument. *Journal of Aggression, Maltreatment & Trauma, 14*, 55−74. Available from http://dx.doi.org/10.1300/J146v14n01_04.

Luft, J., & Ingham, H. (1961). The Johari Window: A graphic model of awareness in interpersonal relations. *Human Relations Training News, 5*(9), 6−7.

Luthans, F., Youssef, C. M., & Avolio, B. J. (2007). *Psychological capital: Developing the human competitive edge.* New York, NY: Oxford University Press.

Luthar, S. S., Cicchetti, D., & Becker, B. (2000). The construct of resilience: A critical evaluation and guidelines for future work. *Child Development, 71*, 543−562. Available from http://dx.doi.org/10.1111/1467-8624.00164.

Maddi, S. R., Harvey, R. H., Khoshaba, D. M., Lu, J. L., Persico, M., & Brow, M. (2006). The personality construct of hardiness, III: Relationships with repression, innovativeness, authoritarianism, and performance. *Journal of Personality, 74*, 575−597. Available from http://dx.doi.org/10.1111/j.1467-6494.2006.00385.x.

Madsen, M. D., & Abell, N. (2010). Trauma Resilience Scale: Validation of protective factors associated with adaptation following violence. *Research on Social Work Practice, 20*, 223−233. Available from http://dx.doi.org/10.1177/1049731509347853.

Masten, A. (2014). *Ordinary magic: Resilience in development.* New York: The Guilford Press.

Masten, A. S., Burt, K. B., Roisman, G. I., Obradović, J., Long, J. D., & Tellegen, A. (2004). Resources and resilience in the transition to adulthood: Continuity and change. *Development and Psychopathology, 16*, 1071−1094.

Masten, A. S., Garmezy, N., Tellegen, A., Pellegrini, D. S., Larkin, K., & Larsen, A. (1988). Competence and stress in school children: The moderating effects of individual and family qualities. *Journal of Child Psychology and Psychiatry, 29*, 745−764.

Masten, A. S., Hubbard, J. J., Gest, S. D., Tellegen, A., Garmezy, N., & Ramirez, M. (1999). Competence in the context of adversity: Pathways to resilience and maladaptation from childhood to late adolescence. *Development and Psychopathology, 11*, 143−169.

Motowildo, S., & Beier, M. E. (2010). Differentiating specific job knowledge from implicit trait policies in procedural knowledge measured by a situational judgment test. *Journal of Applied Psychology, 95*, 321−333. Available from http://dx.doi.org/10.1037/a0017975.

Pangallo, A., Zibarras, L., Lewis, R., & Flaxman, P. (2015). Resilience through the lens of interactionism: A systematic review. *Psychological Assessment, 27*(1), 1−20. Available from http://dx.doi.org.ezproxylocal.library.nova.edu/10.1037/pas0000024.

Pellegrini, D. S., Masten, A. S., Garmezy, N., & Ferrarese, M. J. (1987). Correlates of social and academic competence in middle childhood. *Journal of Child Psychology and Psychiatry, 28*, 699−714.

Prince-Embury, S. (2008). The resiliency scales for children and adolescents, psychological symptoms, and clinical status in adolescents. *Canadian Journal of School Psychology*, *23* (1), 41–56. Available from http://dx.doi.org/10.1177/082957350816592.

Rutter, M. (2006). Implications of resilience concepts for scientific understanding. *Annals of the New York Academy of Sciences*, *1094*, 1–12. Available from http://dx.doi.org/ 10.1196/annals.1376.002.

Ryan, L., & Caltabiano, M. (2009). Development of a new resilience scale: The Resilience in Midlife Scale (RIM Scale). *Asian Social Science*, *5*, 39–51. Available from http://dx.doi.org/10.5539/ass.v5n11p39.

Shaffer, A., Coffino, B., Boelcke-Stennes, K., & Masten, A. S. (2007). From urban girls to resilient women: Studying adaptation across development in the context of adversity. In B. J. R. Leadbeater, & N. Way (Eds.), *Urban girls revisited: Building strengths* (pp. 53–72). New York: New York University Press.

Sinclair, V. G., & Wallston, K. A. (2004). The development and psychometric evaluation of the Brief Resilient Coping Scale. *Assessment*, *11*, 94–101. Available from http:// dx.doi.org/10.1177/1073191103258144.

Smith, B. W., Dalen, J., Wiggins, K., Tooley, E., Christopher, P., & Bernard, J. (2008). The brief resilience scale: Assessing the ability to bounce back. *International Journal of Behavioral Medicine*, *15*, 194–200. Available from http://dx.doi.org/10.1080/ 10705500802222972.

Southwick, S. M., & Charney, D. S. (2012). *Resilience: The science of mastering life's greatest challenges*. Cambridge, UK: Cambridge University Press.

Vaishnavi, S., Connor, K., & Davidson, J. R. T. (2007). An abbreviated version of the Connor-Davidson Resilience Scale (CD-RISC), the CDRISC2: Psychometric properties and applications in psychopharmacological trials. *Psychiatry Research*, *152*, 293–297. Available from http://dx.doi.org/10.1016/j.psychres.2007.01.006.

Vanderbilt-Adriance, E., & Shaw, D. S. (2008). Conceptualizing and re-evaluating resilience across levels of risk, time, and domains of competence. *Clinical Child and Family Psychology Review*, *11*, 30–58. Available from http://dx.doi.org/10.1007/s10567-008-0031-2.

Wagnild, G. M., & Young, H. M. (1993). Development and psychometric evaluation of the Resilience Scale. *Journal of Nursing Measurement*, *1*, 165–178.

Windle, G. (2011). What is resilience? A review and concept analysis. *Reviews in Clinical Gerontology*, *21*(02), 152–169. Available from http://dx.doi.org/10.1017/ S0959259810000420.

Wright, M. O., Masten, A. S., & Narayan, A. J. (2013). *Resilience processes in development: Four waves of research on positive adaptation in the context of adversity* . *Handbook of resilience in children* (2nd ed., pp. 15–37). New York: Springer Science + Business Media. Available from http://dx.doi.org.ezproxylocal.library.nova.edu/10.1007/978-1-4614-3661-4_2.

CHAPTER 3

Family Resilience: Coping With the Unexpected

Abstract

This chapter is dedicated to the family. First, the role of childhood development is explored, including the outcomes of breakdowns in caring, family maladaptations, and the role of anger in the family. Then, three major stressors are outlined—environmental trauma, economic disturbance, and medical/mental health trauma. Within these domains, the authors specifically focus on the effects that these types of trauma have upon family units. Given that interpersonal roles reorganize following trauma, relationships must be redefined. The critical need for family therapy is discussed. First, people must have time to grieve and begin the healing process. It is important to note, however, that healing does not necessarily mean returning to premorbid functioning. As such, the role of acceptance is crucial in assisting people in moving forward.

Keywords: Family stressors; coping; environment; trauma; rehabilitation; phases of recovery

Contents

Innovative Approaches to Individual and Community Resilience
DOI: http://dx.doi.org/10.1016/B978-0-12-803851-2.00003-9

"Much of resilience, especially in children, but also throughout the life-span, is embedded in close relationships with other people" (Southwick, Bonanno, Masten, Panter-Brick, & Yehuda, 2014, p. 5). These relation-ships begin with attachment to the mother, then they expand slowly to include the father, other siblings, and people outside the nuclear family. Much has been written about the quality of the mother–child relationship as being a major predictor of how these children handle unexpected diffi-culties in their adult lives. In fact, 90% of people tend to experience major stressors during their lifetime (The Science of Resilience and How It Can Be Learned, 2015). Some of these stressors can be expected, like the birth of a sibling or death of a grandparent; others, however, can be sudden and quite unexpected, like an external event or an internal event. External events may include, but are not limited to, such things as envi-ronmental problems, societal unrest, and/or economic difficulties. Internal events, however, primarily focus on an individual's state of health and/or well-being.

PHYSICAL, EMOTIONAL, AND SPIRITUAL DISTRESS

These events, if not properly handled, can result in physical, emotional, and spiritual distress. In describing the people he saw on the streets of New York one morning while walking to work, Harville Hendrix (1992) noted the following observations:

> I was struck by how few people appeared happy or relaxed. Nearly everyone seemed to be carrying a burden that broadcast itself in...expression, ...stride, ...body language; careworn old women stooped by loss and loneliness; middle-aged men with grim, guarded faces off to their jobs, carrying lunch boxes or briefcases; melancholy, defiant teenagers, purposeless on a summer morning; exhausted, anxious mothers bringing their children to daycare — even their young children already bore signs of the losses and tragedies their lives had dealt them. The occasional vibrant or content passerby was almost a jar-ring exception. I wondered what showed in my own face.
> Taken aback by the apparent pain and injury all around me, I thought about how we all come to this moment in life, wearing on our sleeves the toll

exacted by disappointment and sorrow, the wear and tear of anger and loss and fear. Yet each of us started life relaxed and whole and joyful (pp. 51—52).

What Hendrix described several decades ago holds true today. Few people are thriving. Most are just wandering through life—anxious, depressed, torn apart by grief and sorrow—unprepared for and devastated by the *unexpected.* Does it have to be this way? Where are the vibrant, content passersby? Is it really possible to not only survive, but to *thrive*?

THE EMOTIONAL IMPACT OF MAJOR STRESSORS

We believe that it is possible to thrive, despite the challenges that arise from the unexpected. This chapter, therefore, focuses on the emotional impact of major internal or external stressors that families experience. Resilient families tend to fair much better when confronted with major stressors, than non-resilient families. Some families willingly accept change, while others have a more difficult time doing so (Ruddy & McDaniel, 2016). Somehow, resilient families find a way of adapting to these stressful events; whereas families that lack resilience tend to fall apart.

According to Bowlby (1969), "The process of becoming adapted refers to a change of structure" (p. 51). Bowlby explains that there are two types of changes that can occur. "First, a structure can be changed so that it continues to attain the same outcome but in a different environment. Secondly, a structure can be changed so that it attains a different outcome in the same or similar environment" (p. 51). When an unexpected event occurs, a change of structure is required. It is not always easy for families to manage this adaptation. At first, families are shocked by the event. Once that sense of shock passes and the acute stage of the experience comes to a close, families are often left in a state of bewilderment, not knowing what to do or how to proceed. We will explore three examples of this dynamic process; but first, we must discuss the role of *children's development* as they attempt to *develop resilience.*

A DEVELOPMENTAL APPROACH TO RESILIENCE

Hendrix (1992) outlines six important stages of development that children experience. These stages, along with the accompanying age ranges, are as follows: attachment (0—18 months), exploration (18—36 months), identity (3—4 years), competence (4—7 years), concern (7—13 years), and intimacy (13−19 years). Nemeth, Ray, and Schexnayder (2003) hypothe-sized that, during each of these stages, children have specific emotional needs that must be met, which include the following (in developmental order): attachment security, attention, acceptance, approval, acknowledg-ment, and affection. As they locomote these stages, Hendrix (1992) notes that children are encouraged to believe that they have a right to exist, that the world is a wonderful place, that they can be who they are (e.g., *I am me*), that they can succeed, that they belong, and that they can be close and loving. Table 3.1, which summarizes these concepts, is provided below.

When children are allowed to be heard, positive, understood, success-ful, considered, and related, they develop an amazing sense of resilience; however, not all children are raised in happy, healthy families. According to Murphy and Oberlin (2001), there are often family maladaptive experiences that children suffer during their developmental years. According to Hendrix's developmental stages, these families can feel fran-tic, angry, troubled, defective, lonely, and indulgent, which lead to anger and breakdowns in caring. In these dysfunctional families, anger is dis-played via stress, power plays, pain, embarrassment, sadness, and/or exces-sive desire. This dysfunction results in such breakdowns in caring at times, that children may often experience being abandoned, intimidated, rejected, abused, neglected, and/or betrayed. Such experiences underlie children's lack of resilience to manage the stressors they face, in childhood as well as in adulthood. Table 3.2 summarizes the breakdowns in caring that occur developmentally; their outcomes; family maladaptations; and the role of anger.

Table 3.1 Developmental stages, emotional needs, and messages (Hendrix, 1992; Nemeth et al., 2003)

Developmental stages	Emotional needs	Messages
1 Attachment (0−18 months)	Attachment security	"I have a right to exist/be here."
2 Exploration (18−36 months)	Attention	"I see the world as wonderful and exciting."
3 Identity (3−4 years)	Acceptance	"This is me (who I am)."
4 Competence (4−7 years)	Approval	"I can do it (succeed)."
5 Concern (7−13 years)	Acknowledgment	"I belong here."
6 Intimacy (13−19 years)	Affection	"I can be close and loving."

Table 3.2 Breakdowns in caring and associated outcomes

Stages	Breakdowns in caring	Painful outcomes	Family maladaptations	Role of anger
1	Abandonment	Manipulation	Frantic	Stress
2	Intimidation	Isolation	Angry	Power
3	Rejection	Conditional love	Troubled	Pain
4	Abuse	Reaction	Defective	Embarrassment
5	Neglect	Control	Lonely	Sadness
6	Betrayal	Mistrust	Indulgent	Desire

ENVIRONMENTAL TRAUMA

"There appears to be a universal six-state process that follows environmental trauma. These six stages are as follows: shock, survival mode, basic needs, awareness of loss, susceptibility to spin and fraud, and resolution" (Nemeth & Whittington, 2012, p. 120). Whether it is the result of a hurricane, such as Katrina, or an oil spill, such as the 2010 Deepwater Horizon/British Petroleum (BP) incident, shock, which can be defined as a reaction to "sudden physical or mental disturbance," occurs (Campbell, 1981, p. 583). Then, people must figure out what it takes to survive. After managing this step, it is necessary that they reassess how they are going to proceed and what they need in order to move forward. Being aware of their losses occurs shortly after the assessment of needs. Just when families seem to take a minute to reconnect and rebuild, they often need to turn to others for help. This is when the spin and fraud begins. Regardless of the nature of the stressor, there are usually people in the immediate horizon who are willing to take advantage of the situation. After navigating this quagmire, then movement toward resolution takes place. Resolution is hardly immediate. It can take a long time; very seldom does it happen quickly. There are many problems that families encounter along the way. Furthermore, resolution does not always lead to a happy ending. Many families do not survive the awareness of loss, let alone the susceptibility to spin and fraud, to experience a happy ending.

Societal Resilience

It is important to take a moment to define resilience within the context of these environmental disasters. Colten, Grimsmore, and Simms (2015) offer the following definition of resilience: "Resilience, at least in the realm of social sciences, means the ability of a society to absorb the impacts of an external disturbance, to recover and rebuild itself to a functional state (National Academy of Sciences, 2012)" (p. 392). This definition points out the importance of planning and organizing for external disturbances. In this regard, Tom Wilbanks (2008) defines a resilient community "as one that anticipates problems, opportunities, and potentials for surprises; reduces vulnerabilities related to development paths, socioeconomic conditions, and sensitivities to possible threats; responds effectively, fairly, and legitimately in the event of an emergency; and recovers rapidly, better, safer, and fairer" (p. 10). Colten et al. (2015) cite the importance of perceiving resilience as a process, not an outcome. They then explore the differences between "inherent resilience" (bottom–up) and "formal resilience" (top-down) (p. 392). In top-down programs to promote resilience, they "focus on three elements: anticipate, reduce, and respond" (p. 392).

Long-Term Resilience

As in all areas of trauma, Colten et al. (2015) highlight the fact that long-term resilience has often been neglected. Basically, they point out the need for intervention long after the crisis has passed. We agree that this intervention is needed, especially for families and communities, long after the immediate crisis has passed, regardless of the source of the trauma (e.g., environmental, economic, and/or health issues). Colten and colleagues outline three major categories of inherent resilience: networks, mobility, and ingenuity/adaptation. They point out that locally-based response and recovery efforts usually begin long before formal interventions arrive (i.e., Civil Defense and/or Red Cross). Furthermore, Colten et al. state that geographic and economic mobility often allows families and communities to "persist in place" (2015, p. 394). They point out how the use of raised homes post-Katrina allows coastal areas to survive storm surges and that temporary migration inland can help with adaptation and survival. They emphasize that the family support structure is a crucial variable in resilience.

When faced with litigation, as often follows oil spills, class action lawsuits are usually formed; however, uneven damage awards frequently received by litigants tend to undermine community resilience and "contribute towards the creation of a 'corrosive community' (Fredenberg, 1997; Picou et al., 2004)" (Colten et al., 2015, p. 399). Furthermore, Colten et al. conclude that, "Unlike hurricane resilience, there has been a stark disjunction between formal and inherent practices for oil spills" (p. 400). Therefore, although collective action through formal organizations can be very helpful, the authors note that local action through community networks can be very powerful and effective. Colten et al. also suggest that, in response to any disaster, "the rapid mobilization of aid as a factor in reducing individual stress and aiding community wellbeing" is crucial (2015, p. 402). The authors then conclude that, "despite efforts to foster community resilience in the context of 'multi-hazards,' there is a glaring distinction between the impacts and uncertainties of hurricanes and human-made disruptions such as oil spills and diversions. Coastal residents and communities are accustomed to hurricanes and proclaim a capacity to absorb the blow from these meteorological events" (Colten et al., 2015, p. 403). They then review comparative analyses, which suggest that "technical hazards produce more psychological stress than natural events" (Colten et al., 2015, p. 403). This was verified by Onishi, Voitsekhovich, and Zheleznyak (2007) in their book *Chernobyl What Have We Learned? The Successes and Failures to Mitigate Water Contamination Over 20 Years.*

Technical Versus Natural Disasters

Perhaps people tend to perceive technical disasters to be more preventable, such as the BP oil spill (Streitfeld, 2011); whereas natural disasters, often referred to as *acts of God*, are more expected. Although this may arguably be true, many of the *outcomes* of natural disasters can be prevented. On December 1, 2001, an article was published in the *Houston Chronicle* noting the likelihood of a hurricane of disastrous proportions striking New Orleans (Berger, 2005, *republished from 2001*). Subsequently, in the October 2004 edition of *National Geographic*, Bourne, Jr., described "a broiling August afternoon in New Orleans, Louisiana," in which a storm "with the fury of a nuclear warhead [pushed] a deadly storm surge into Lake Pontchartrain" (para. 1). "When did this calamity happen?" Bourne, Jr., writes (para. 5). "It hasn't—yet. But the doomsday scenario is not far-fetched. The Federal Emergency Management Agency lists a hurricane strike on New Orleans as one of the most dire threats to the nation, up there with a large earthquake in California or a terrorist attack on New York City. Even the Red Cross no longer opens hurricane shelters in the city, claiming the risk to its workers too great" (para. 5).

Many would argue that the powers that be rely primarily on numbers when making decisions. We would argue, however, that although this perception may be logical, it is not necessarily factual. According to *Scientific American*, Louisiana's "entire plan of more than 100 recommended projects to revitalize the delta region is estimated to cost a separate $50 billion" (Fischetti, 2015, para. 19). Estimates of Hurricane Katrina's damages, however, ranged from $96 to $125 billion, with most of the damage occurring after the storm had been reclassified from a category five to a category three storm (Amadeo, 2016). In discussing the Fukushima Daiichi nuclear power plant, Onishi (2012) points out that the plant was not designed to withstand earthquakes and tsunamis. Instead, he notes that "It is important to select appropriate design condition levels by considering consequences when beyond-the-design conditions occur" (pp. 26–27). He explains that all the Japanese nuclear power plants "are now required to install systems to avoid plantwide electric blackouts in the event of beyond-design tsunamis or other unexpected long-term electrical failure" (p. 27). Similarly, on a local level, Louisiana State University has begun to showcase a model house that is better equipped to handle disasters such as hurricanes (Wold, 2016).

Death Versus Closure

How do these facts impact families? Even with all the life lost post-Hurricane Katrina (i.e., approximately 1833 deaths, according to Dall, 2015) the 11 lives lost in the BP explosion and oil spill were perceived by many as more egregious. Clearly, these deaths could have been prevented. As Colten et al. (2015) describe, crises produced by technical hazards have more long-lasting impacts than do natural events. For one thing, natural events may not lead to litigation. People might be upset with their government officials or insurance companies, or other agencies, but they seldom sue. Rather, they take action to better plan and prepare for the next event. Most do not abandon their cities and/or homes. Their sense of belonging (i.e., oikophilia) is too strong. For example, a local women's organization, *Women of the Storm*, was formed post-Katrina to lobby Congress and foster awareness of the poor funding of rebuilding efforts in Louisiana (Advocate Staff Report, 2015). These women made quite a statement by carrying blue umbrellas representing the iconic blue tarps that covered damaged buildings following the hurricane.

In spite of all the deaths and despair, families did their best to reunite as quickly as possible and rebuild; nevertheless, a decade after Katrina,

30 bodies have yet to be identified (Dall, 2015). Arguably, however, the State's response to this tragic loss of life likely facilitated closure. As Dall (2015) pointed out, "State health officials say the department spent more than $3 million in an effort to reunite families with the remains of their deceased relatives" (para. 18). Conversely, with the BP oil spill, litigation was prolonged, and many families were unable to seek closure. For example, some bodies were unable to be retrieved, and some families had to wait seven years before receiving a formal death certificate (Schleifstein, 2013).

What perhaps was most disturbing, however, was the disregard for human life, the suffering the victims' families experienced, and the catastrophic effects of the disaster upon the environment that was perpetrated by some in corporate America. The then-chief executive officer of BP, Tony Hayward, for example, after apologizing for the incident, was noted to have told reporters that he would like to have his life back (Snyder, 2010). Later, when asked how he could sleep at night knowing of the disastrous effects of the oil spill, Hayward was quoted as responding, "Of course I can" (Snyder, 2010, para. 10). Although the victims' families were clear that no amount of compensation could make up for their terrible losses, it was undoubtedly difficult to know that, while they were awaiting resolution, Mr. Hayward "[walked] away with a full year's salary and a $900,000-a-year pension" (Editorial Board, 2010, para. 4). Such inequitable resolutions and/or prolongations prevented closure. These families, as well as the families of some Katrina victims, remained in limbo for longer than the typical five-year grieving period.

Without closure, families have a very difficult time moving on. Healthy families will somehow endure, whereas fractured families will not. Furthermore, when families are impacted by trauma, they tend to regress to their developmental stage that is filled with unfinished business (see Table 3.2). For example, some families regress all the way back to Stage 1 and become frantic. Other families are consumed with anger. Many families become extremely troubled and in need of mental health intervention, and defective families fall apart. These families that are unable to remain together emotionally separate into very lonely parts. Lastly, some families become quite indulgent and members may turn to alcohol or substance abuse for comfort. These breakdowns in caring are frequently the result of a lack of closure. It is very difficult for families to retain resilience when closure is not forthcoming.

ECONOMIC DISTURBANCE

Throughout the world, when economic hardships occur, regardless of etiology, families struggle. No amount of resilience can protect a family from loss of a job, loss of opportunity, loss of available resources, loss of homeland. Currently, many wars are raging throughout the world. This is causing a major migration of refugees to other countries that has not been experienced since the second World War (Nordland, 2015). When refugees escape from the burdens of their homeland, they are often forced to leave families behind or to experience family separations. Currently, the impact of the immigrants from the Middle East (i.e., mostly Syria, Afghanistan, and Iraq), according to a report by the British Broadcasting Corporation (BBC, 2016, "Migrant crisis"), on Africa and Europe, is enormous. If, indeed, people survive their journeys, with the goal of seeking a better, safer life, they are often met with disdain. Many perish in their travels, especially across the Mediterranean Sea. In fact, the BBC describes April 2015 as the deadliest month for immigrants, during which time a boat carrying 800 people capsized off of the coast of Libya (BBC, 2016). Others are held up in refugee camps (e.g., Greece), overburdening the local economy.

Societal Integration

This flood of refugees, due to economic instability and life threatening situations, has caused more societal problems than ever before. How can these people be integrated into their new countries? Where are these people going to work? What kind of social support can they expect?

On a global level, this is currently leading to chaos. Yet, on a local level, the same problems abound. For example, in Baton Rouge, Louisiana, since the 2016 shootings, societal/racial tensions have been enormous. More important, however, has been the history of the lack of opportunity afforded to African-Americans for jobs, education, and respect. Just as refugees from Africa and the Middle East are experiencing few available opportunities, so are many of our minority citizens in the United States.

A Cry for Change

The recent riots in Baton Rouge are not only a reaction to the local shootings, but they are also a cry for change. Integrating minority members into the society as a whole is crucial to the overall well-being of that society. When an African-American woman states that she is afraid that her teenage son might not come home at night (personal communication, June 12, 2015), how can a family survive and thrive? Yet, the goal of resilience is to promote thoughts and behaviors that allow people to survive and thrive. As sad as it is to know what the African and Middle Eastern refugees are experiencing, it is even sadder to realize that such struggles are right at our own backdoor. Many African-American families have sought refuge in faith-based organizations. These serve as valuable networks. Without mobility, as Colten et al. (2015) point out, how can there be adaptive ingenuity? Much must be done to help minority citizens experience the same opportunities that majority citizens take for granted every day.

Incomplete Families

One observation is that minority families may often be incomplete. Frequently, grandmothers are raising grandchildren. Oftentimes mothers are working two and three jobs to make ends meet, and children, especially adolescents, turn to inappropriate role models for guidance. This unraveling of African-American families can be found in the roots of slavery, where families were separated and sold for monetary gain. In fact, several prestigious universities, "including Brown, Columbia, Harvard, and the University of Virginia—have publicly recognized their ties to slavery and the slave trade" (Swarns, 2016, para. 5). Recent research has uncovered the fact that, in the fall of 1838, Jesuit priests in Maryland sold 272 slaves to plantation owners in the Deep South for a sum of what would be equivalent to about $3.3 million today. Reportedly, this was done to prevent Georgetown University from a financial disaster (Swarns, 2016). Throughout this process, many families were separated, sent to different plantations, and not allowed to practice their Catholic faith. Thus, even when institutions were supposedly devoted to family values, they had a history of defying these values for economic gain. It is taking centuries for African-American families to recover from these ungodly acts.

Now, a new wave of minorities is coming from the Middle East and Africa. How will these families fare? The integrity of the family is crucial to resilience and well-being.

MEDICAL AND MENTAL HEALTH TRAUMA

As Muriel Lezak so eloquently wrote nearly 30 years ago, brain injury is a family affair (Lezak, 1988). This is true not only about brain injury, but often about any major medical or mental health illness to inflict a family member. Brain traumas are often, if not always, unanticipated, snatching people by surprise and challenging their realities. In discussing chronic illness, Ruddy and McDaniel (2016) point out that it is not unlike an unwanted guest who overstays his welcome. It creates chaos, disturbs typical routines, causes stress, and leaves families with a high degree of uncertainty.

Oftentimes, medical and mental health illnesses, including chronic illnesses, can result in insults to that which makes a person unique. Brain injuries, for example, usually result in cognitive, emotional, and personality alterations. As such, marital, parental, and parent–child relationships are often strained, leading to a cascade of difficulties for families. Similarly, spinal cord injuries can affect various aspects of physical and cognitive functioning, which can greatly impact marital relationships. As such, families are faced with having to adjust not only to the effects of the illness or trauma, but also to the psychological fallout that subsequently occurs (Ruddy & McDaniel, 2016). It is important, therefore, that the "hidden side" of what families are likely to experience surrounding the injury of a loved one be revealed. As the authors' main focus is on the rehabilitation of those who have suffered brain injuries, this section will primarily focus on this type of trauma.

The Economic Costs

According to the Centers for Disease Control and Prevention (2016), 2.5 million cases of traumatic brain injury were recorded in 2010. Recent self-report surveys indicated that over 40% of individuals will experience a traumatic brain injury during their lifetime (Whiteneck, Cuthbert, Corrigan, & Bogner, 2016). In 2012, chronic illness affected about 50% of Americans and accounted for over 80% of healthcare dollars (Mechanick & Kushner, 2016). Likewise, mental health disorders are no exception. Of those with a mental health diagnosis, 4.5% are hospitalized, with bipolar patients hospitalized at a much higher rate—39.1% (Centers for Disease Control and Prevention, 2013). These experiences undoubtedly take a toll on all aspects of a family.

The Emotional Costs

We believe that these experiences are quite traumatic for families and result in a cascade of challenges that are rarely adequately addressed or supported. Families need help in both the acute and postacute phases; but help is seldom available, and if it is available, it is not always able to be accessed.

Ruddy and McDaniel (2016) outline several adaptations with which the family is faced during these stressful times. First, family members' roles are usually forced to change to care for the injured or ill family member, requiring a great deal of flexibility from the family. Second, many families tend, either consciously or inadvertently, to assign the role of primary caregiver to one or two select individuals. The more shared the responsibility, the more distributed the burden, the easier it is to cope with trauma. It is quite difficult, however, when the burden falls upon one caregiver. Additionally, caregivers may find it hard to ask others for help, and quickly dwindling resources further compound existing challenges. Third, illness/injury can have a significant financial effect upon the affected individual, given that occupational functioning is often impacted. These implications can be even more overwhelming if the head of the household, or "primary wage earner," as Ruddy and McDaniel describe (p. 473), is unable to maintain employment. Fourth, treatment costs include both money *and time*, which require adjustments in all of the family members' schedules. Ruddy and McDaniel explain that these changes may range from small to very elaborate:

> For example, the family may need to integrate time-consuming treatment regimens into their every day routines. The varying levels of willingness and ability to make such changes amongst family members can create enormous tension (McDaniel & Cole-Kelly, 2003). Well family members may feel resentment as they make difficult changes to assist the ill member of the family. Some family members may willingly embrace necessary changes while others struggle. It is not uncommon for family members to interpret the attitudes toward success with such changes as an indication of loyalty to the ill family member and/or to the family itself (2016, p. 473).

Lastly, families may struggle with the issue of how much they should willingly disclose to others. This can be particularly difficult with illnesses such as substance abuse, brain injury traumas that occurred due to unscrupulous acts (e.g., illegal activity), and medical conditions that may still be poorly understood by many (e.g., fibromyalgia and many other chronic pain conditions).

It is important to understand that these families are facing a multitude of losses simultaneously (Ruddy & McDaniel, 2016). On the other hand, some of these losses evolve over time. Initially, the family may be so focused on the acute care of the injured/ill individual, that other effects, such as those discussed above, are not realized until some time has passed.

The Four Phases of Recovery

In the following paragraphs, we outline four phases of recovery. It is important to note, however, that these phases may not be mutually exclusive and are rarely clearly delineated.

Acute Injury Phase I

In the initial phase of injury, families are often blindsided by the trauma. Examples include a major motor vehicle accident, cancer diagnosis, attempted suicide, diagnosis of severe mental illness (e.g., schizophrenia), complications from substance abuse, brain injury (e.g., cerebrovascular accidents, traumatic brain injuries), injuries from improvised explosive device explosions, spinal cord injury, or a wide variety of other types of medical/mental health issues. Families are often in shock at this point, and the primary focus surrounds providing urgent care to the injured or compromised individual. For some, however, this phase may be more insidious in nature and therefore associated with a slower onset of symptoms. During this phase, in addition to acute medical and/or mental health care, the family is primarily in need of social support.

Acute Injury Phase II

After the individual's medical and/or mental health status has stabilized, the acute phase may extend to include an inpatient hospitalization of several days to several months. During this time, the individual may be in a state of altered consciousness (e.g., coma, vegetative state, minimally conscious state), despite being deemed medically stable. This is often confusing and difficult for the family to understand. This stage represents a time of extended acute stress for family and caregivers. Family members may be away from their homes and other loved ones for several days, weeks, or months. Hospitals (especially smaller, more rural ones) are often ill-equipped to accommodate overnight family stays, and family members may find themselves sleeping in chairs, or on floors and windowsills in waiting areas to be close to their loved one. Aspects of life that are normally taken for granted on a daily basis may become difficult to navigate. For example, it can be expensive to eat out for every meal while staying with a loved one in the hospital. What if there is no cafeteria available? For those with an extensive social network, they might find that friends may offer to bring meals to the hospital; but what about those without such support? Oftentimes, family members are found scavenging for meals at the vending machines. Poor nutrition and inadequate sleep further exacerbate physical and emotional stress. During this phase, especially for those with limited external support, things like daily showers, checking the mail, paying bills, etc., are often not done in a timely manner. Personal hygiene is often a luxury, and bills are likely to become delinquent.

Rehabilitation

In essence, rehabilitation is a lifelong process for many individuals. Initially, however, it can reasonably be considered a two-part process. More severe injuries will often lead to an inpatient rehabilitation admission following the acute care phase. This admission can range from several weeks to several months, depending on a number of factors such as the nature and extent of the injury, prognosis, treatment goals, treatment progress, and unfortunately, reimbursement/managed care issues. Outpatient services often follow inpatient rehabilitation.

During this phase, the individual and family face numerous unique logistical challenges. Arguably, the most salient challenges for many people include a lack of awareness of treatment options and difficulty accessing such resources. For example, in very rural and underserved areas of the United States, inpatient rehabilitation facilities are not offered as treatment options as they are simply not available geographically. Therefore, people may find themselves discharged to home or to a nursing facility (e.g., if more specialized care is required, such as a tracheotomy and ventilator, or feeding tubes). Alternatively, some individuals may be discharged with follow-up appointments to medical providers and outpatient rehabilitation services. Although these services are valuable and quite effective for a number of people, this level of care may be insufficient for individuals with more severe injuries and/or geographically unfeasible, resulting in a number of missed appointments. Oftentimes, it is the mental health clinician's responsibility to provide these individuals with assistance in locating inpatient rehabilitation facilities. Perhaps a psychologist, mental health counselor, or social worker may be assigned this role.

The Psychosocial Stressors

Psychosocially, stressors become more apparent during this phase, although they may still not be at the center of concern. These include financial difficulties due to loss of work for both the individual and the family members; extended absences from school for children and young adults; temporary relocations; and health coverage issues due to loss of work and/or income. Furthermore, due to extended hospitalizations and the intensive nature of rehabilitation care, both the individual and the family members may experience decreased social interaction. Parents may find that they have less time to spend with children, who often have to rely on care from other family members and friends. Additionally, it is not uncommon to see many families bringing all aspects of their lives into rehabilitation facilities, such as birthday and anniversary celebrations and homework instruction (i.e., usually for children and adolescents).

Emotionally, if memory permits, individuals and their family members may begin to process the traumatic event and its consequences on a deeper level. Although some individuals may still be in the "initial shock" phase, many may start to realize—even if on a very rudimentary level—that life is different now. That is, life is different for the individual, and life is different for all of the family members. Sometimes rehabilitation treatment goals are lofty, yet attainable, such as relearning how to walk after a spinal cord injury. Some goals, however, are more functional in nature, such as working toward more consolidated sleep/wake cycles, learning how to effectively comply with bowel and bladder programs, using assistive technology devices for communication, and/or learning how to use a wheelchair for mobility.

Transitioning Home and Ongoing Rehabilitation

Within the context of inpatient rehabilitation settings, it is not uncommon for individuals and practitioners to have different definitions of *treatment goals*. In fact, common perceptions among people and their families include beliefs such as, *I will be discharged when I have fully recovered from my injuries; I will be able to walk out of here;* or *I will not go home with a tracheostomy/ventilator.* While in many cases these hopes are realized, there are a number of individuals for whom this will not be the case. Careful consideration, therefore, must be given to the individual's and family's understanding of realistic treatment goals and expectations for discharge.

Upon discharge, individuals may have a comprehensive outpatient treatment plan already set up for them. Oftentimes, this is completed by nurse case managers or other treatment team members in advance of discharge. At other times, however, individuals and their families may be faced with a number of logistical responsibilities, such as setting up outpatient physical therapy, occupational therapy, speech and language therapy, and follow-up medical appointments. Furthermore, transitions back to work and/or school, if applicable, can also be difficult to navigate. This is especially true if additional assistance is required (e.g., special accommodations, vocational rehabilitation, Individualized Education Programs, or 504 Plans).

Altered Lives

From a psychosocial perspective, change has occurred. Individuals whose lives have been altered may find it difficult to transition back into their previous home, work, school, and/or social settings. Many times, people have been removed from such settings for several weeks to months, and reintegration can be both physically and emotionally challenging given their individual needs. For example, if individuals were discharged with otherwise novel medical equipment (e.g., tracheostomy/ventilators, oxygen, wheelchairs, walkers, canes, assistive technology for communication), this can make home and community reintegration very complex. They must find a way to adapt and move forward, and so must their families.

Emotionally and behaviorally, the individual may be subject to both direct and indirect problems following brain injury. Lezak (1988) outlines the direct consequences as including impaired social perception and social awareness, impaired control, dependency, an inability to learn from experience, and specific emotional alterations of a structural nature (e.g., apathy, childishness, increased reactivity, and irritability). Indirect consequences include emotional difficulties due to the perceived trauma of the injury (e.g., anxiety, depression) and paranoia as a result of "perceptual inaccuracy coupled with a lack of insight, feelings of worthlessness because of incompetencies, and fears of rejection because of those incompetencies" (p. 120). As a result, family dynamics often shift dramatically in a relatively short period of time, causing considerable strain, especially upon spouses and/or caregivers.

Burdened Families

In discussing the work of Thomsen (1992), Perlesz, Kinsella, and Crowe (1999) point out that "personality and emotional changes in the head-injured person contributed more to family burden than did the physical and cognitive changes" (p. 12). It is also important to understand that the subjective burden, which is "the amount of strain or distress experienced by the relative as arising from these 'objective' changes [i.e., changes observed in the injured individual]," (McKinlay, Brooks, Bond, Martinage, & Marshall, 1981, p. 529) appears to increase as time passes.

Although these researchers focus primarily on head injury, the results arguably have important implications for a wide variety of major medical/mental health traumas. As Perlesz et al. (1999) state,

> The pattern of burden in relatives over the period of follow-up indicated that within 3 months after trauma, 69% of relatives reported a medium to high level of burden or strain in caring for the head-injured person and that this proportion gradually increased over time. At 6 months, 73% of relatives reported at least this level of burden, and this level was sustained at 12 months for 75% of relatives. At 5 years after trauma, the proportion of relatives experiencing this level of strain had increased to 89% and remained at 89% up to 7 years following the TBI (Brooks et al., 1986, 1987; McKinlay et al., 1981) (p. 12).

Oftentimes, when stabilized and released from inpatient care, individuals and their families are given a rosy picture of what the next few years might bring, but as the aforementioned researchers point out, that is not always the expected outcome. Individuals who have suffered severe trauma, especially brain trauma, have often lost social skills and connectedness. Research, however, indicates that "improvement in psychosocial functions can continue for several years" (Thomsen, 1984, p. 268). This is important given that psychological changes post-trauma are likely to have the greatest impact upon the family. Therefore, the focus of rehabilitation must shift. This is precisely why effective family psychotherapy, following a major trauma, is crucial.

THE CRITICAL NEED FOR FAMILY THERAPY

Researchers have documented the importance of *reconstruction* following major injury or trauma (Couchman, McMahon, Kelly, & Ponsford, 2014; Levack, Kayes, & Fadyl, 2010). Such reconstruction is undoubtedly important on an individual level (e.g., self-identity, personhood, sense of belonging; Levack et al., 2010). We conclude, however, that reconstruction is just as crucial on a family level. Furthermore, Couchman et al. (2014) discuss how building a "new normal" through themes of connectedness, identity, and knowledge and understanding can help individuals and families navigate the post-trauma period (p. 817). This is important for children, their parents, and the family as a whole. Regarding promoting resilience within the family as a whole, Jordan and Salorio (2015) note that "children cannot be considered in isolation from their family system" (p. 18), emphasizing the importance of psychological care for all members of the family.

Perhaps the most salient support for family therapy surrounds the fact that premorbid family characteristics, whether positive or negative, are often exacerbated following trauma. As Ruddy and McDaniel (2016) explain,

The stress of an illness can serve to pull a somewhat disengaged family together or heighten tensions in an already struggling family. Pre-existing patterns of communication and roles often become more rigid when the family is stressed by illness. The pre-illness role of the ill family member impacts how stressed the family is by the potential loss of function, and how able they are to replace the functions that person is no longer able to perform. (p. 474).

All too often, it seems that families are more inclined to fall apart following trauma rather than to be pulled closer together. This is heartbreaking and further adds to the "multiple losses" the family has already experienced. Family therapy, however, is a resource than can help hurting families navigate the terrain of trauma and illness and support their ability to not just survive, but to thrive.

Mental health professionals are well poised to address the many changes that occur in the lives of individuals and families following traumatic events. As Bechtold (2015) points out, "The ultimate goal is to assist individuals with brain injury in returning to fulfilling and engaged lives... [yet,] access to high-level brain injury professionals and services is not always available and general providers do not necessarily have access to information for understanding the needs of individuals with brain injury, regardless of severity" (p. 6). During and following rehabilitation and resolution, individuals and their families are in desperate need of the services provided by qualified professionals, including mental health practitioners. In fact, it could be argued that mental health clinicians may be most influential in helping individuals and families achieve and maintain resilience throughout these difficult years. Furthermore, ensuring continuity of care is paramount, and clinicians are encouraged to follow up with families throughout rehabilitation and beyond discharge into the first few years of recovery.

Barriers to Treatment

One of the problems with this intervention model is finances. Most cannot afford these services, and managed care is not generous in this regard. In order to facilitate meaningful recovery and pursue functional gains, family relationships will need to be redefined. At a higher, more systemic level, policy reform must address the way in which these services are reimbursed.

A second issue with this type of intervention, as discussed above, concerns the mental health professionals. Many professionals are well trained and experienced in addressing *mental health*, but may find themselves struggling to address more medically-based traumas and illnesses. A statement common among doctoral-level mental health professionals is, "But I'm not a medical doctor!" In describing the value and need for medical family therapy, however, Ruddy and McDaniel (2016) explain that practitioners must be willing and able to traverse "the largely separate worlds of mental healthcare and medical care" (p. 474). Too often, practitioners operate in silos, but this is an antiquated and ineffective model of healthcare. Integrated models have been proposed for quite some time, not only in more traditional medical fields, but in psychology as well. As Mann (2005) stated, we need to move "from silos to seamless healthcare" (p. 34). This requires a concerted effort for increased practitioner collaboration, which is sometimes not initiated due to time and effort demands. Furthermore, practitioners often feel restricted from communicating with other healthcare professionals without written consent from the patient in advance (i.e., due to Health Insurance Portability and Accountability Act [HIPAA] regulations), which is not always feasible to obtain.

Necessary Family Adjustments

Following trauma and/or illness, family members' lives are forever changed. As previously discussed, there is a tremendous initial burden, multiple losses, and long-term issues that must be carefully addressed. As such, families are faced with a choice—they can either adapt and move forward, or they can become stuck. Family therapy can be a catalyst to assist with these most difficult adjustments, adaptations, and changes, and the therapist can serve as an essential guide throughout the journey.

Ruddy and McDaniel (2016) outline the following strategies that therapists can utilize to help families adapt to illness and move forward (adapted from p. 476). They are as follows:

1. Increase awareness of changing family roles (e.g., practical, emotional),
2. Assist with implementing major family lifestyle changes (e.g., cessation of unhealthy habits, changing diets, consistently adhering to treatment regimens),
3. Foster healthy communication about the illness/trauma within and outside of the family,

4. Support the family in letting go of things they cannot control and instead, putting effort toward areas in which they can make a difference,

5. Discover meaning,

6. Foster grieving of multiple losses (e.g., physical, emotional),

7. Facilitate collaboration between family members and among the treatment team,

8. Address previous family experiences with illness and loss, and

9. Create goals that can help the family to accept, grieve, heal, and move forward.

Acceptance and Moving Forward

A considerable amount of grief accompanies brain injury recovery. One of the primary challenges for the individual and family will be to deal with this grief effectively. Acceptance is essential and is a catalyst for change; yet, grieving must come first. Dr. Henry Cloud, psychologist and author of *Necessary Endings*, outlined the grieving process as follows:

> The grieving process is a mental and emotional letting go. What that means is to face the reality that it is over, whatever it is, and to feel the feelings involved in facing that reality. It means to come out of the denial and numbness emotionally and feel whatever you feel. The reason that helps, though, is that grief has movement to it. It goes somewhere. It goes forward. Feeling the anger helps get the protest out of the way, and feeling the sadness helps move the letting go further along. It gets people unstuck. When people do not feel their feelings, positive and negative, about something significant that has ended, they will remain tethered to it in some way.
>
> That is why the feelings involved in grief are unique. Unlike emotions that do not take us anywhere and in fact can keep us stuck, the feelings of grief have forward motion to them. When you feel grief, you are saying, "I am looking this reality right in the face and dealing with it, the reality that this [whatever this is] is over. Finished. Grief also means I am getting ready for what is next, because I am finishing what is over" (Cloud, 2010, p. 213).

Unfortunately, a number of individuals eventually find themselves stuck and unable to move forward. Why is this? Why are some people able to move on and experience posttraumatic growth, while others decline—physically, emotionally, and, perhaps, spiritually? As Cloud observed, honoring the grieving process is essential. Yes, grief has forward motion, but it will only move individuals forward if they trust in the process (oftentimes, they may need permission from an authority figure to do so). Eventually, grieving gives way to acceptance: acceptance of the altered self, the altered life, the altered family, and the altered situation.

An important part of acceptance is appreciation: appreciation for surviving, for the love of family and friends, and perhaps, for God. For those who subscribe to religious or spiritual beliefs, these concepts can provide a sense of meaning because faith, hope, and love play an important role in recovery (Daaleman & Frey, 2004; Jang & LaMendola, 2007; Zelinski, 2013). Somehow, functional families can find a way to do this. Dysfunctional families, however, tend to turn on one another, project blame, and fall apart.

REFERENCES

Advocate Staff Report. (2015, March 11). Documentary on women of the storm debuts Thursday, Feb. 26 at the Prytania. *The Advocate*. Retrieved from http://www.theadvocate.com/new_orleans/entertainment_life/movies_tv/article_3d715f81-651d-5dd7-9f2d-9b87567a7012.html.

Amadeo, K. (2016, May). *Hurricane Katrina facts: Damage and economic effects*. Retrieved from http://useconomy.about.com/od/grossdomesticproduct/f/katrina_damage.htm.

BBC. (2016, March 4). Migrant crisis: Migration to Europe explained in seven charts. *British Broadcasting Corporation*. Retrieved from http://www.bbc.com/news/world-europe-34131911.

Bechtold, K. (Ed.) (2015). Guest editor's message. *Brain Injury*, *12*(3), 6, 8.

Berger, E. (2005). The foretelling of a deadly disaster in New Orleans. *The Houston Chronicle*.

Bourne, J. K., Jr. (2004). Gone with the water. *National Geographic*, *206*(4), 88−105. Retrieved from http://ngm.nationalgeographic.com/ngm/0410/feature5/.

Bowlby, J. (1969). *Attachment and loss* (Vol. 1New York: Basic Books.

Campbell, R. J. (1981). *Psychiatric dictionary* (5th ed.). New York: Oxford University Press.

Centers for Disease Control and Prevention. (2013, October 4). *Burden of mental illness*. Retrieved from https://www.cdc.gov/mentalhealth/basics/burden.htm.

Centers for Disease Control and Prevention. (2016, January 22). *TBI: Get the facts*. Retrieved from http://www.cdc.gov/traumaticbraininjury/get_the_facts.html.

Cloud, H. (2010). *Necessary endings: The employees, businesses, and relationships that all of us have to give up in order to move forward*. New York: Harper-Collins Publishers.

Colten, C. E., Grimsmore, A. A., & Simms, J. R. (2015). Oil spills and community resilience: Uneven impacts and protection in historical perspective. *Geographical Review*, *105*(4), 391−407.

Couchman, G., McMahon, G., Kelly, A., & Ponsford, J. (2014). A new kind of normal: Qualitative accounts of multifamily group therapy for acquired brain injury. *Neuropsychological Rehabilitation*, *24*(6), 809−832. Available from http://dx.doi.org/10.1080/09602011.2014.912957.

Daaleman, T. P., & Frey, B. B. (2004). The Spirituality Index of Well-Being: A new instrument for health-related quality-of-life research. *The Annals of Family Medicine*, *2*(5), 499−503.

Dall, T. (2015, August 27). Bodies remain unidentified decade after Katrina. *USA Today*. Retrieved from http://www.usatoday.com/story/news/nation/2015/08/27/bodies-remain-unidentified-decade-after-katrina/32474355/.

Editorial Board. (2010, July 28). Good-bye and good riddance to Tony Hayward, BP's gaffe master: An editorial. *The Times-Picayune*. Retrieved from http://www.nola.com/news/gulf-oil-spill/index.ssf/2010/07/good-bye_and_good_riddance_to.html.

Fischetti, M. (2015, August). Is New Orleans safer today than when Katrina hit 10 years ago? *Scientific American*. Retrieved from http://www.scientificamerican.com/article/is-new-orleans-safer-today-than-when-katrina-hit-10-years-ago/#.

Hendrix, H. (1992). *Keeping the love you find*. New York: Atria Books.

Jang, L. J., & LaMendola, W. (2007). Social work in natural disasters: The case of spirituality and post-traumatic growth. *Advances in Social Work, 8*(2), 305–316.

Jordan, L., & Salorio, C. (2015). Resiliency in children: Considerations after pediatric traumatic brain injury (TBI). *Brain Injury Professional, 12*(3), 18–21.

Levack, W. M., Kayes, N. M., & Fadyl, J. K. (2010). Experience of recovery and outcome following traumatic brain injury: A metasynthesis of qualitative research. *Disability and Rehabilitation, 32*(12), 986–999.

Knowles, P. (2009). Collaborative communication between psychologists and primary care providers. *Journal of Clinical Psychology in Medical Settings, 16*(1), 72–76.

Lezak, M. (1988). Brain damage is a family affair. *Journal of Clinical and Experimental Neuropsychology, 10*(1), 111–123. Available from http://dx.doi.org/10.1080/01688638808405098.

Mann, L. (2005). From "silos" to seamless healthcare: Bringing hospitals and GPs back together again. *Medical Journal of Australia, 182*(1), 34–37.

McKinlay, W. W., Brooks, D. N., Bond, M. R., Martinage, D. P., & Marshall, M. M. (1981). The short-term outcome of severe blunt head injury as reported by relatives of the injured persons. *Journal of Neurology, Neurosurgery & Psychiatry, 44*(6), 527–533.

Mechanick, J. I., & Kushner, R. F. (2016). The problem: Chronic disease. In J. I. Mechanic, & R. F. Kushner (Eds.), *Lifestyle medicine: A manual for clinical practice* (pp. 1–8).

Murphy, T., & Oberlin, L. H. (2001). *The angry child: Regaining control when your child is out of control*. New York: Clarkson Potter Publishers.

Nemeth, D. G., & Whittington, L. T. (2012). Our robust people. In D. Nemeth, R. Hamilton, & J. Kuriansky (Eds.), *Living in an environmentally traumatized world: Healing ourselves and our planet* (pp. 113–140). Santa Barbara, CA: Praeger.

Nemeth, D. G., Ray, K. P., & Schexnayder, M. M. (2003). *Helping your angry child: Worksheets, fun puzzles, and engaging games to help you communicate better*. Oakland, CA: New Harbinger Publications, Inc.

Nordland, R. (2015, October 31). A mass migration crisis, and it may yet get worse. *The New York Times*. Retrieved from http://www.nytimes.com/2015/11/01/world/europe/a-mass-migration-crisis-and-it-may-yet-get-worse.html.

Onishi, Y. (2012). Our living waters: Polluting or cleansing? In D. Nemeth, R. Hamilton, & J. Kuriansky (Eds.), *Living in an environmentally traumatized world: Healing ourselves and our planet* (pp. 23–39). Santa Barbara: Praeger.

Onishi, Y., Voitsekhovich, O. V., & Zheleznyak, M. J. (2007). *Chernobyl—What have we learned? The successes and failures to mitigate water contamination over 20 years*. Dordrecht: Springer.

Perlesz, A., Kinsella, G., & Crowe, S. (1999). Impact of traumatic brain injury on the family: A critical review. *Rehabilitation Psychology, 44*(1), 6–35. Available from http://dx.doi.org.ezproxylocal.library.nova.edu/10.1037/0090-5550.44.1.6.

Ruddy, N., & McDaniel, S. H. (2016). Medical family therapy. In T. L. Sexton, & J. Lebow (Eds.), *Handbook of family therapy* (pp. 471–483). New York: Routledge.

Schleifstein, M. (2013, January 15). Family members of BP Deepwater Horizon accident victims criticize company's $4.5 billion criminal settlement. *The Times-Picayune*. Retrieved from http://www.nola.com/news/gulf-oil-spill/index.ssf/2013/01/family_members_of_bp_deepwater.html.

Snyder, B. (2010, June 10). Tony Hayward's greatest hits. *Fortune*. Retrieved from http://archive.fortune.com/2010/06/10/news/companies/tony_hayward_quotes.fortune/index.htm.

Southwick, S., Bonanno, G., Masten, A., Panter-Brick, C., & Yehuda, R. (2014). Resilience definitions, theory, and challenges: Interdisciplinary perspectives. *European Journal of Psychotraumatology, 5.* Available from http://dx.doi.org/10.3402/ejpt.v5.25338.

Streitfeld, R. (2011, January). *Panel calls for drastic steps to stop future deepwater oil spills.* Retrieved from http://www.cnn.com/2011/US/01/11/gulf.oil.spill.report/#.

Swarns, R. L. (2016, April 16). 272 slaves were sold to save Georgetown. What does it owe their descendants? *The New York Times.* Retrieved from http://www.nytimes.com/2016/04/17/us/georgetown-university-search-for-slave-descendants.html?_r = 0.

The Science of Resilience and How It Can Be Learned [Audio blog interview]. (2015, August 25). Retrieved July 18, 2016, from http://thedianerehmshow.org/shows/2015-08-24/the-science-of-resilience-and-how-it-can-be-learned.

Thomsen, I. V. (1984). Late outcome of very severe blunt head trauma: A 10-15 year second follow-up. *Journal of Neurology, Neurosurgery & Psychiatry, 47*(3), 260–268.

Whiteneck, G. G., Cuthbert, J. P., Corrigan, J. D., & Bogner, J. A. (2016). Prevalence of self-reported lifetime history of traumatic brain injury and associated disability: A statewide population-based survey. *The Journal of Head Trauma Rehabilitation, 31*(1), E55–E62. Available from http://dx.doi.org/10.1097/HTR.0000000000000140.

Thomsen, I. V. (1992). Late psychosocial outcome in severe traumatic brain injury. *Scandinavian Journal of Rehabilitation Medicine, Supplement, 26,* 142–152.

Wilbanks, T. (2008). Enhancing the resilience of communities to natural and other hazards: What we know and what we can do. *Natural Hazards Observer, 32*(5), 10–11.

Wold, A. (2016, July 18). Learn about making homes stronger against floods and hurricanes at LaHouse Saturday. *The Advocate.* Retrieved from http://www.theadvocate.com/baton_rouge/news/environment/article_32cb7fd2-4d39-11e6-a4bc-2f1f1cc33775.html.

Zelinski, S. (2013). Our critical issues in coping with environmental changes: The intersection of nature, psychology, and spirituality. In D. Nemeth, R. Hamilton, & J. Kuriansky (Eds.), *Living in an environmentally traumatized world: Healing ourselves and our planet* (pp. 169–178). Santa Barbara, CA: Praeger.

CHAPTER 4

Community Resilience: Baton Rouge—A Community in Crisis— Grieving and Moving Forward

Abstract

Chapter 4 recounts situations of devastation and loss that led to community resilience. The example of the Louisiana Great Flood of 2016, following the racial strife subsequent to a shooting earlier that summer, resulted in a fragmented community coming together to help one another.

The text describes experiential learning opportunities along with six stages of environmental trauma: shock, survival mode, assessment of basic needs, awareness of loss, susceptibility to spin and fraud, and resolution. Group healing situations are depicted, and the term resilience is defined at a community level.

The memories of a devastating event, with lingering willingness to help others, are shown to be powerful forces that coalesce to change collective behavior, and create collective memory. The healing process is illustrated through example, with references to intervention, children's needs, and group dynamics. A discussion of the importance of blending psychology and spirituality to create resilience is included.

Keywords: Resilience; intervention; experiential learning; environmental trauma; group dynamics

Contents

Innovative Approaches to Individual and Community Resilience
DOI: http://dx.doi.org/10.1016/B978-0-12-803851-2.00004-0

By early August 2016, my coauthor, Traci Olivier, PsyD, had left Baton Rouge, Louisiana, for Memphis, Tennessee, to begin her postdoctoral fellowship at St. Jude Children's Research Hospital in Pediatric Neuropsychology. I had just returned from the American Psychological Association's Annual Convention in Denver, Colorado, and was preparing to write this chapter.

Then... Wham... the skies opened up and for three days, August 12–14, 2016, over 31 inches of rain fell on the Greater Baton Rouge area. Those who were not flooded out, were, like me, flooded in. There was no escape. For days, I was glued to the television (yes, we did have electricity!) watching neighborhood after neighborhood go under. Six feet of water here. Eight feet there. Traci's family home was within a few inches of being lost; several of her husband's family were completed flooded and forced to evacuate. As our home was on a hill, we were safe—but cut off from everything and everyone.

I could not go anywhere. I felt helpless. Then, the survivor's guilt set in. I should be doing something. But what?

Neighbors in the flooded areas began helping one another. People with small boats came from all over Louisiana to help rescue people. At that moment, through technology and the efforts of creator Rob Gaudet, the "Cajun Navy" was born. According to *Louisiana Life* magazine, "Gaudet applied his tech savvy... to help with the effort to organize a floating rescue militia of boat-owning volunteers." Gaudet stated "through hundreds of boats, we saved thousands of people... but technology really enabled it" (Kalec, 2017, para. 6).

It did not matter if you were black or white, rich or poor, young or old, person or pet—all were joined together in a common cause—that of saving our community. Considering the racial strife secondary to the Alton Sterling shooting death earlier that summer (Lou & Stole, 2016), coming together to help one another was truly a blessing.

A LOCAL TRAGEDY

Although the Alton Sterling shooting death and the racial protests that followed made ongoing national news, Louisiana's Great Flood of 2016 did not. Most people living elsewhere barely knew it existed. Yet, locally, this environmental trauma was, and still is, overwhelming.

Many elderly woke up the first night of the Great Flood in a bed surrounded by water. Nursing homes, let alone houses, had to be evacuated. There was no place to go. Emergency shelters were quickly opened, only to be closed because the waters were approaching. Schools, churches, businesses all flooded. Almost the entire downtown area of Denham Springs, Louisiana, and nearby shopping centers were inundated with water (Kinchen, 2016).

PETS, PICTURES, AND PROOF

When people were asked what they took with them, most said that they took their pets. When asked what they regretted leaving behind, most replied that it was their family photos. So many important documents were lost. Still to this day, some flood victims cannot prove that they own their homes. In Louisiana, many homes and properties were just passed down through the generations. But in order to get help, people must have proof. Titles? Deeds? What is that? For some, proof of ownership has become an impossible situation. So, of course, no help was available to them.

THE GOVERNOR AND THE MEDIA

It was very painful watching families go through the Six Stages of Environmental Trauma: (1) Shock, (2) Survival Mode, (3) Assessment of Basic Needs, (4) Awareness of Loss, (5) Susceptibility to Spin and Fraud, and (6) Resolution (Nemeth & Whittington, 2012). Local media did an excellent job of helping people to understand this process. In fact, local media coverage throughout this entire ordeal was excellent. So was the Governor. Governor John Bel Edwards, newly elected in his first year of office, was everywhere doing whatever he could to calm people down and assure them that help was on the way. The Governor and his staff worked tirelessly to mobilize local, state, and federal resources to help (Crisp, 2016).

When people came out of shock and began to experience the pain of their losses, Governor Edwards was there to acknowledge their pain and to offer the reassurance that only a compassionate authority figure can offer. He did so with empathy, compassion, and understanding—for he was flooded too! Yes, the entire basement of the Governor's Mansion, which held all of the computers and communication networks, was wiped out (Associated Press, 2016). The Governor and his family had to move out while repairs were made. So they too knew firsthand how it felt to be displaced.

RESILIENCE: A NEW HOUSEHOLD WORD

Resilience became a new household word overnight. Although schools were closed and life was topsy-turvy, people were not giving up. They were helping one another and fighting to rebuild their homes and their very lives. People who did not ever know one another were helping to tear out sheetrock and flooring so that repairs could begin.

SPIN AND FRAUD

And then there is the Spin and Fraud. The news media, the Governor's office, and the Attorney General's Office were all on top of this, providing information about spotting fraudulent contractors and how to protect oneself from them. Although some overly eager homeowners did end up getting "ripped off" by such people, most did not. Another blessing.

IT SHOULD NOT BE THIS HARD

Local and state governments rose to the challenge. Although the Federal Emergency Management Agency (FEMA) was better in its response to this disaster than to Hurricane Katrina, there were still problems. For example, applying for a FEMA trailer was very complicated. Furthermore, when one was available, a $33,000 trailer often ended up costing more like $100,000 when all the hidden costs were assessed (Allen, 2016). Perhaps the federal government could have just given all flooded homeowners $100,000 and let them figure it out (McCollister, 2017). As one home owner told an *Advocate* reporter, "It shouldn't be this hard" (Griggs, 2016).

A DOUBLE BIND

At one point, between FEMA, various mortgage companies, and attempting to self-contract to save money, many homeowners found themselves in a double bind. Of the 58,000 homes that were damaged by the August 2016 Great Flood, according to an article in *The Advocate* on December 19, 2016 "only one in eight was covered by flood insurance..." when "they were not in federally established flood zones where insurance is required to get a mortgage" (Marshall, 2016, p. 4A). So, if flood insurance was not required, most (unlike my husband Donald, who is an Environmental Geologist) did not get it. So, many were left without coverage.

THE PLIGHT OF THE SENIORS

And then there were the seniors. Many, like several of my friends, lived in older homes in the Sherwood Forest area of Baton Rouge. Like many other seniors, these friends had long since retired their mortgage and themselves. Their home, which was completely paid for, would cost so much to repair, that they just walked away, sold it "as is," and moved out of state, near their daughter. Although they now live in an apartment, at least they do not have to deal with "all that rig-a-marol." Other seniors, who did not have family out of state, were lucky enough to find apartments locally; yet, many do not expect to own their own home ever again.

NO PLACE TO GO

But many are not so fortunate. They have no place to go. Their families are here. Their jobs are here. Their schools are here. They just have to "deal with it," so to speak.

THE NEED FOR EMOTIONAL INTERVENTION

Once again, the "Louisiana Spirit Crisis Counseling Program," which was staffed with a 24-hour hotline, social workers, counselors, etc., provided assistance for those who needed emotional support. This program, funded by FEMA, cosponsored our Hurricane Katrina Anniversary Wellness Workshops in 2006 (Nemeth et al., 2012).

Likewise, when the Louisiana Psychological Association (LPA) rose to the occasion to offer Emotional Resiliency Workshops.[1] Staff members

---

[1] Workshop materials are available for non-profit use to others who are conducting emotional resiliency interventions. They may be obtained by contacting Darlyne G. Nemeth Ph.D., M.P., M.P.A.P. at dgnemeth@gmail.com

from the Louisiana Spirit Program were there to help! More information regarding this program can be obtained from louisianaspiritinfo@la.gov.

But why offer these experiential learning opportunities? It is my firm belief that, when a tragedy happens to a group, it must be dealt with in a group. The healing power of a group cannot be underestimated. This healing process, which is neither counseling nor psychotherapy, is an amazing phenomenon. It worked in the Hurricane Katrina Anniversary Wellness Workshops (Nemeth et al., 2012).

As their capacity to think logically is diminished and/or overwhelmed by their feelings, emotionally traumatized people will become increasingly vulnerable and make many mistakes post-trauma. They will try to settle claims too quickly or fall for various schemes or, as my friends did, just walk away. The approaching holidays (e.g., Thanksgiving and Christmas), which merely enhanced their feeling of loss, seemed to be an ideal time for the Emotional Resiliency Workshops.

THE INTERVENTION COMMITTEE

Considerable planning is involved in any meaningful intervention projects. A committee, cochaired by Charles Burchell, PhD, and myself, was initiated by LPA. Dr. Burchell and I were psychology doctoral students together at Louisiana State University many years ago. Dr. Burchell went on to have a successful career in police psychology and I in group dynamics and neuropsychology. The committee consisted of six members with specifically assigned tasks: Fernando Pastrana, PhD (research), T. Shavaun Sam, PhD (lunches), Andrew Yarborough, PhD (ministers), Valaray Irvin, PhD (facilitators), student member Stedwin Coleman, MS (workshop location), and LPA Executive Director, Cindy Bishop (Beanie Babies® bears). Altogether, our group was ethnically diverse, consisting of four African Americans, three Caucasians, and one Hispanic psychologist. The committee was originally formed to address the social unrest following the shooting death of Alton Sterling by local police and the subsequent ambush of four police officers, three of whom died and one of whom suffered severe brain damage. It turned out that this police shooter came from another state to intentionally create chaos. A significant protest, widely covered by the national and local news media, ensued (Lou & Stole, 2016).

With Dr. Burchell's experience as a police psychologist and mine as a group psychotherapist, we began to create interventions to address community concerns. Among other intervention strategies, we had intended to use Fisher, Ury, and Patton's *Getting to Yes* Model (1991, p. 68).

But then came the Great Flood! Some said that it was a great equalizer, affecting all alike. Other more religious people, suggested that it was God's way of bringing people together to address what was really important—Resilience! No matter what the belief or ideology, the outcome was that the word *resilience* was now on everyone's lips. As helping others is a cornerstone of a healthy community, people from all walks of life began figuring out what they could do to help. And they did it! From the "Cajun Navy" to the "Louisiana Spirit" ... from local churches, like the Florida Boulevard Baptist Church, which hosted our workshops, to the Celtic Movie Studios, which housed so many in need. Since the Salvation Army Headquarters was flooded, St. Vincent de Paul stepped in to join forces to help. Clothes, blankets, toys, etc., were donated by individuals and groups. People volunteered to staff the shelters, cook food,

Figure 4.1 Flyer.

and offer accommodations. Together the state and federal governments paid for hotel rooms and apartments for many. But, most people just wanted to go home. The gutting of the flooded houses by so many community volunteers, most of whose names remain unknown, was the real treasure. With a bathtub, a bed, and a Christmas tree, many families celebrated the holidays in their own homes with gratitude. In spite of the turbulent summer, their community spirit was alive and well.

Thus, our Emotional Resiliency workshops were just one of many interventions developed by local people to help one another. During the workshops, which were organized by my two clinical assistants, LaJae Coleman, BS, and Kortney Wooten, BS, people had an opportunity to share their feelings, be affirmed, reprioritize their needs, problem-solve, and implement resilient strategies to move forward (Fig. 4.1).

INFORMED CONSENT AND CONFIDENTIALITY

In order to facilitate these experiences, the Centre model was employed to create psychological safety in groups (Cave, Pearson, Whitehead, & Rahim-Jamal, 2016). Thus, at the beginning of each three-hour session, participants were asked to sign a Resiliency Workshop Release (Fig. 4.2). The group coordinator then explained the concepts of (1) Experiential Learning, (2) Confidentiality, (3) Voluntary Participation, and (4) Research. If children were present, parents were asked to give consent on their behalf.

RESEARCH

Each participant received a folder that included pre- and post-intervention questionnaires. One of which was from the Resiliency Resource Centre—for either adults, teens, or children (Child and Youth Resiliency Measure-28)—and the other was created by Nemeth and Pastrana to gather some demographic data and measure anxious and sad feelings (Fig. 4.3).

FEELINGS

As stated earlier in this chapter, environmentally traumatized people must first sort out and address their feelings before effective problem-solving can occur. Therefore, the concept of "regression in the service of the

Resiliency Workshop Release
Hold Harmless Release for Adults, Teens, and Children

A) Experiential Learning

I understand and acknowledge that this is an experiential learning workshop, and not a form of counseling or therapy; as such, no doctor-patient or counselor-patient relationship exists. I further understand that this experiential learning workshop is based on a wellness model of group intervention. This model is designed to teach people how to develop a better perspective for themselves as they endeavor to cope with the aftermath of the Great Flood of 2016. Thus, I understand that this is a teaching model for people who are dealing with difficult life experiences.

B) Confidentiality

I understand and agree that, during the course of this group experience, people may share very personal information. In order for this experience to be a safe and comforting one, I agree to leave the personal sharings of others in the group. I understand, however, that anything I wish to share about my own experiences and/or what I learned, I am free to do so.

C) Voluntary Participation

I understand that my participation in this workshop is completely voluntary. I agree to defend, release and hold harmless all individuals and sponsors who are offering/leading this workshop. I also agree to hold harmless the facility in which this workshop is held.

D) Research

I understand that any data gathered from this workshop may be used as a part of a clinical and/or scientific presentation. When this is done, no information which could specifically identify me will be shared.

By signing this release, I acknowledge the aforecited stipulations for either myself or my child/teen.

Name of Participant:_____

If a minor, name of parent: _____

Date of Workshop:_____

Signature:_____

Figure 4.2 Workshop Release.

THE GREAT FLOOD 2016 RESILIENCY WORKSHOP INFORMATION SHEET

ID #: _____A   AGE: _____   TODAY'S DATE: _____

AREA OF RESIDENCE DURING THE FLOOD: _____

ETHNICITY:
- ☐ African American
- ☐ Asian American
- ☐ Caucasian
- ☐ Latino
- ☐ Creole
- ☐ Other

EDUCATION:
- ☐ 0 - 12 years
- ☐ 13 – 16 years
- ☐ 17+ years

MARITAL STATUS:
- ☐ Single
- ☐ Co – Habitating
- ☐ Married
- ☐ Widowed
- ☐ Divorced

DWELLING:
- ☐ Owns home/ Condo
- ☐ Renting house/ Condo
- ☐ Apartment
- ☐ Other: _____

TEMPORARY HOUSING:
- ☐ Mobile Home/ Camper
- ☐ Hotel/ Motel
- ☐ Relative Friend
- ☐ Shelter at Home
- ☐ Not Applicable

INSURANCE:
- ☐ Dwelling
- ☐ Vehicle
- ☐ Business
- ☐ None

Resiliency Questionnaire (Pre)

How much are you currently experiencing:

0 = Not at all   1= A little bit   2 = Moderately   3 = Quite a bit   4 = Extremely

1. Loss of interest in closeness.	0 1 2 3 4
2. Getting irritated easily.	0 1 2 3 4
3. Thoughts of giving up.	0 1 2 3 4
4. Fighting back tears.	0 1 2 3 4
5. Feeling overwhelmed.	0 1 2 3 4
6. Blaming anyone and everyone.	0 1 2 3 4
7. Feeling helpless and alone.	0 1 2 3 4
8. Feeling sad.	0 1 2 3 4
9. Worrying about rebuilding.	0 1 2 3 4
10. Lacking joy.	0 1 2 3 4
11. Not seeing a solution.	0 1 2 3 4
12. Not having the strength to endure.	0 1 2 3 4
13. Feeling unimportant.	0 1 2 3 4
14. Nervous feelings.	0 1 2 3 4
15. Shaking.	0 1 2 3 4
16. Being frightened easily.	0 1 2 3 4
17. Feeling afraid.	0 1 2 3 4
18. Heart palpitations.	0 1 2 3 4
19. Being on "red alert."	0 1 2 3 4
20. Panicking.	0 1 2 3 4
21. Feeling agitated.	0 1 2 3 4
22. Fearing the future.	0 1 2 3 4
23. Frightening thoughts or dreams.	0 1 2 3 4

Figure 4.3 Nemeth & Pastrana's Resiliency Workshop Information Sheet and Resiliency Questionnaire.

ego" (Gold, 2011) was utilized in order to assist participants in correctly recognizing, labeling, and sharing their feelings. In our society of mixed and/or confusing signals, this step was considered to be extremely important. For example, scared children are often told not to be scared, etc. It was, therefore, considered important that all feelings be allowed.

RILEE BEAR TO THE RESCUE

In my first book, *Helping Your Angry Child* (2003), which was coauthored with Kelly Paulk Ray and Maydel Morin Schexnayder, the concept of RILEE Bear was used (Fig. 4.4) to make sure that all readers were able to correctly identify six basic feelings: angry, happy, scared, sad, embarrassed, and anxious. Dr. Kelly Ray, representing the World Council for Psychotherapy, was present at one of the workshops to model this process. Bear faces were used in the book and subsequently in the workshops because of their universal appeal.

Not only was RILEE Bear (which stands for Relating In Love Every Evening) implemented to reframe emotional expression, he was also utilized to offer a relaxation exercise to assist participants in feeling

Figure 4.4 RILEE Bear (*Relating in Love Every Evening*).

more comfortable and safe both while at the workshops and afterward. Recordings were tailored to both adults and children. Dr. Burchell became the voice of RILEE Bear. All participants received a recorded copy of the exercise on their e-mail (as many did not have current addresses, e-mails were gathered instead). Participants found it easy to relax in the soft sound of Dr. Burchell's voice. In fact, several weeks after one of the adult workshops, a participant told me that she uses the

RILEE Relaxation Exercise for the Great Flood of 2016

Darlyne G. Nemeth, Ph.D., M.P., M.P.A.P.

Hi, I am RILEE Bear, your friendly relaxation bear.
RILEE stands for "Relating in Love Every Evening"

Since the great flood last August, being calm has been very hard to do.
Like you, my house was flooded, too.

I was so scared. The water kept rising.
I didn't know what to do.

My family kept each other safe.
But, every now and then, I still think of that scary night when the waters kept rising.

Sometimes, I even dream about it.
But, dreams are just fantasies.
They are not real.

So, I have learned to calm myself down before going to bed.
By telling myself that, "I can feel comfortable and safe, any time, any place."

As I say my prayers, I ask God to "Keep me safe every night and every day."
Like He did the night of the Great Flood.

Since the Great Flood, I have learned that
For every loss, there is hope
For every set back, there is strength,
And for every challenge, there is resilience

I am resilient and I am safe.

Since the Great Flood, I have also learned that
Home is where our hearts are
And that when our hearts are connected in love, we are safe

When we love and are loved,
We are safe

When we are scared, we feel alone, lost, and afraid.
We are not safe.

When we connect, we feel safe.

Remember, safety is a matter of the heart.
But, comfort is a matter of the mind.
Both are gifts we give ourselves.
One by loving and connecting
And the other by calming ourselves down, and thinking good thoughts.

By taking care of myself and managing my worries and fears,
I can Relate in Love Every Evening and
I want to share these secrets with you.

This way you can feel comfortable and safe
Any time any place,
Just like me, RILEE Bear.

Even as a big powerful bear, I need support and that's okay.
So, while you are in your chair, let yourself feel the chair, press down on the chair,
And know that you are safe.

The way I do this is to breathe deeply.
So, let's practice breathing deeply together.

First, I want you to put a big smile on your face and a twinkle in your eyes –
One – two – three –
Now, take a deep breath
Puff out your cheek with air.
Count to five on your fingers.
One, two, three, four, five.
And let that breath out slowly.

Let's do it again.

First, I want you to put a big smile on your face and a twinkle in your eyes –
One – two – three –
Now, take a deep breath
Puff out your cheek with air.
Count to five on your fingers.
One, two, three, four, five.
And let that breath out slowly.

Figure 4.5 RILEE Relaxation Exercise for Adults.

If you do this four times in a row, you will begin to feel relaxed, very, very relaxed, very, very safe

That's what I, RILEE Bear, do to feel safe.
And, when I breathe deeply,
I think of happy days ahead.
So now, you know that, by breathing deeply and slowly
And by choosing good thoughts,
You, too, can feel comfy and safe any time, any place

Now, let's think the opposite – let's remember the flood.

The other day I went back to my house,
All my things were on the curb—
Wet and ruined.
I touched them and instantly remembered that horrible night when the waters rose
Just a few inches
Then a few feet
The waters kept coming and coming
I was so scared.

I noticed that my heart was pounding,
My breathing was shallow,
And I was panting, panting, panting.
I put my paw in front of my mouth.
My breath was so hot
I thought I was on fire.
It was a nightmare all over again!
So now, close your eyes, and let's pretend that you, like me, RILEE Bear
Went back to your house
Remembering the waters rising, needing to leave quickly
Knowing that nothing would be the same when you returned
And noticed that your heart was pounding
Your breathing was shallow and when you put your hand in front of your mouth,
Your breath was hot, hot, hot.
In fact, your breath was so hot, that you thought you were on fire.

But NO!—it was just the intense, intense, sunlight
Just like me, you learned that you did not need your possessions to keep you safe
Rather, you needed your family, your friends, and your community to help you

And as you remember that night, you remember that you were helped
Whether rescued by truck, or boat, or whatever, you were rescued.
You were brought to safety

Open your eyes.
Now you are back,
And you are rebuilding
You have learned that for every loss, there is hope
For every set back there is strength,
And for every challenge there is resilience.

Like me, you are resilient.
You are grounded in today, you have learned from yesterday,
And you can see yourself in tomorrow.

When you see yourself in tomorrow,
With the help of God, family, and friends
You will get to tomorrow.
Better days are ahead.

Remember again, safety is a matter of the heart.
But, comfort is a matter of the mind.
Both are gifts we give ourselves.
One by loving and connecting
And the other by calming ourselves down, and thinking good thoughts.

When you do this --
You too can feel comfy and safe anytime, any place

Remember, any time you need me,
RILEE Bear,
Just close your eyes, and I'll be there.

Figure 4.5 (Continued).

children's relaxation exercise every night to go to sleep. These interventions were so important, as many had not relaxed for days (Fig. 4.5 (Adults) and Fig. 4.6 (Teens and Kids) contain the scripts for these exercises).

A MORNING BREAK

After the Morning Break, where bottled water and snacks were served, adult participants got down to the hard work of dealing with loss, lessons learned, and rebuilding. They did this in small groups by utilizing

RILEE Relaxation Exercise
for the Great Flood of 2016
Darlyne G. Nemeth, Ph.D., M.P., M.P.A.P.

Hi, I am RILEE, your friendly relaxation bear.
RILEE stands for "Relating in Love Every Evening"

Since the great flood last August, being calm has
been very hard to do.
Like you, my house was flooded, too.

I was so scared. The water kept rising.
I didn't know what to do.

My family kept me safe.
But, every now and then, I still think of that scary
night when the waters kept rising.

Sometimes, I even dream about it.
But, dreams are just fantasies.
They are not real.

So, I have learned to calm myself down before going
to bed.
And I tell myself that, "I can feel comfortable and
safe, any time, any place."

As I say my prayers, I ask God to "Keep me safe every
night and every day." – like He did the night of the
Great Flood.
Since the Great Flood, I have learned that
For every loss, there is hope
For every set back, there is strength,
And for every challenge, there is resilience

I am resilient. I am safe.

Since the Great Flood, I have also learned that
Home is where our hearts are
And that when our hearts are connected in love, we
are safe

When we love and are loved,
We are safe

When we are scared, we feel alone, lost, and afraid.
We are not safe.

When we connect, we are safe.

Remember, safety is a matter of the heart.
But, comfort is a matter of the mind.
Both are gifts we give ourselves.
One by loving and connecting
And the other by calming ourselves down, and
thinking good thoughts.

The way I do this is to breathe deeply.
So, let's practice breathing deeply together.

First, I want you to put a big smile on your face and a
twinkle in your eyes –
One – two – three –
Now, take a deep breath
Puff out your cheek with air.
Count to five on your fingers.
One, two, three, four, five.
And let that breath out slowly.

Let's do it again.

First, I want you to put a big smile on your face and a
twinkle in your eyes –
One – two – three –
Now, take a deep breath
Puff out your cheek with air.
Count to five on your fingers.
One, two, three, four, five.
And let that breath out slowly.

If you do this four times in a row, you will begin to
feel relaxed, very, very relaxed, very, very safe

That's what I, RILEE Bear, do to feel safe.
And, when I breathe deeply,
I think of happy days ahead.
So now, you know that, by breathing deeply and
slowly
And by choosing good thoughts,
You, too, can feel comfy and safe any time, any place

Remember, any time you need me,
RILEE Bear,
Just close your eyes, and I'll be there.

Figure 4.6 RILEE Relaxation Exercise for Children and Adolescents.

individual and community drawings. Several of the adults subsequently attended the children's workshops, where Dr. Judy Kuriansky was present to explain and facilitate her Global Kids Project. "Dr. Judy," as she prefers to be called, is well known for her post-environmental trauma interventions across the globe. This time, she brought pillows made by the children in Haiti (who had recently endured the devastation of Hurricane Matthew) to the children of Baton Rouge (who were currently enduring the devastation of the Great Flood of 2016). As there were more adults and volunteers

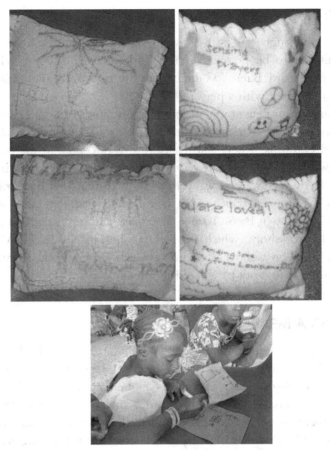

Figure 4.7 Global Kids Project Pillows from Haiti and Louisiana.

at this particular workshop than children, the adults also learned how to create Louisiana pillows for the next group of devastated children. A map was affixed to the wall so that all could gain perspective as to where Haiti was located in relationship to Baton Rouge. As these Louisiana pillows might be sent to Fukushima next, Japan was also located on the map.

EFFECTIVENESS

It was amazing to observe how effective this pillow project was. Participants took great pride in their art work and, more important, in the notion that they could help someone else via this simple creating, sharing project (Fig. 4.7, Haiti pillow, Louisiana pillow).

A CULTURAL BLEND

As Dr. Yarborough was both a psychologist and a minister, he arranged for a minister to be present at each workshop. Workshops, held at the Florida Boulevard Baptist Church courtesy of Ms. Diane Miller, were opened and closed with a prayer.

During times of environmental trauma, psychology and spirituality blend seamlessly to create a resilient union. This is especially true in places like Haiti and Louisiana, where spirituality is so very central to the culture. To create a workshop without this very important component would have been far less effective. This lesson was learned in the original Katrina Anniversary Wellness Workshops, which were held at the Catholic Life Center on Acadian Thruway in Baton Rouge, Louisiana, and reaffirmed in one of the Katrina 10 workshops, which was held at the First Evangelist Missionary Baptist Church on Willow Street in New Orleans, Louisiana. Cultural roots run deep and should not be ignored at time of crisis.

SHARING A MEAL

In a lecture I attended on September 19, 2016 at the Bethany World Prayer Center by an associate researcher, Jenn Ranter, MA, from Wheaton College, on "Helping Children and Teens Cope with Traumatic Events," I learned that traumatized children have to eat and drink something every two hours to help their systems to stabilize. I did not know this. But it made very good sense. Therefore, we included a morning break with snacks and a filling lunch in every workshop. But, the lunches were more than lunch. They provided participants an opportunity to process their experiences in the workshops. It was truly amazing to see how a meal shared can bring people together. Both comfort and safety were present as participants shared their thoughts and feelings and prepared to say goodbye.

Due to the efforts of Dr. Shavaun Sam, lunches were provided by Raising Cane's Chicken Fingers on Corporate Boulevard and the Jambalaya Shoppe in Hammond Aire Shopping Center, both locally well-established restaurants that believe in community service.

GOODBYE

As was the case with the Katrina One Anniversary Wellness Workshops and Katrina 10 Workshops, many participants did not complete their postworkshop forms. Most, however, verbally shared that the workshops were helpful. Some even chose to return for another workshop experience. As the Louisiana Spirit Volunteers who attended the workshops had also been flooded, their data was included with the participants' data. Although the number was small, the positive feedback was enormous. For example, one workshop participant stated, "The workshop allowed me a safe space to be honest about my feelings and my needs." Another stated, "It was very informative and gave us a new and fresh idea to deal with stress." In honor of RILEE Bear participants, young and old, all received Beanie Babies® Bears for attending.

In a perfect world, post-workshop data collection would have been more closely followed. Staff became so caught up in the moment, however, that this was neglected. What was not neglected, however, was the appreciation that all participants conveyed as they said "Goodbye."

POST SCRIPT

The most amazing experience about the aftermath of the Great Flood of 2016 continues to be the outpouring of effort on the part of the individual and collective members of the Greater Baton Rouge community to help those in need. People just do it—either through collective efforts or individuals volunteering to tear out sheetrock or cook food. Practically everyone is doing something. This includes our workshop volunteers, Kortney Wooten, LaJae Coleman, Sonja Washington, Brittany Varmall, Jennifer Robinson, Markenya King, Sarah Bolognino, Margaret Brown, Dianne Miller, Megan Harrison, Jennifer Piscitello, Sarah Ford, Tiffany Augustine, Shaely Cheramie, Jeanette Rimmer, Stedwin Coleman, Rob Mooney, Adrian Scott, and Casey Paulin. That is the mark of a truly resilient community!

REFERENCES

Allen, R. (December 11, 2016). 'It's idiotic': FEMA mobile homes' 6-figure price tags are outrageous, officials say. The Advocate. Retrieved from http://www.theadvocate.com

Associated Press. (2016). Gov. John Bel Edwards hopes to return to flood-damaged Governor's Mansion next month. *The Advocate*. Retrieved from http://www.theadvocate.com

Cave, D., Pearson, H., Whitehead, P., & Rahim-Jamal, S. (2016). CENTRE: Creating psychological safety in groups. *The Clinical Teacher*, *13*(6), 427–431. Available from http://dx.doi.org/10.1111/tct.12465.

Crisp, E. (2016). Gov. John Bel Edwards heads to Washington to pitch $2B flood recovery aid package. *The Advocate*. Retrieved from http://www.theadvocate.com

Fisher, R., Ury, W. L., & Patton, B. (1991). *Getting to yes: Negotiating agreement without giving in.* United Kingdom: Penguin Group.

Gold, J. (2011). *2011: What scientific concept would improve everybody's cognitive toolkit?* Retrieved from https://www.edge.org/response-detail/10539

Griggs, T. (2016). Louisiana homeowners battle red tape, mortgage companies' miscommunications to make flood repairs. *The Advocate.*

Kalec, W. (2017). Louisianians of the year: Community Service—Rob Gaudet. *Louisiana Life.* Retrieved from http://www.myneworleans.com/Louisiana-Life/January-February-2017/Louisianians-of-the-Year/

Kinchen, H. (2016). "It hit everywhere": Denham Springs devastated by record flooding. *The Advocate.* Retrieved from http://www.theadvocate.com

Lou, M., & Stole, B. (2016). "He's got a gun! Gun": Video shows fatal confrontation between Alton Sterling, Baton Rouge police officer. *The Advocate.* Retrieved from http://www.theadvocate.com

McCollister, R. (2017). 'Business Report' publisher: Taxpayers get angry at government waste. *Business Report.* Retrieved from https://www.businessreport.com/

Nemeth, D. G., Kuriansky, J., Reeder, K. P., Lewis, A., Marceaux, K., Whittington, T., et al. (2012). Addressing anniversary reactions of trauma through group process: The Hurricane Katrina anniversary wellness workshops. *International Journal of Group Psychotherapy, 62*(1), 129–142.

Nemeth, D. G., & Whittington, L. T. (2012). Our robust people. In D. Nemeth, R. Hamilton, & J. Kuriansky (Eds.), *Living in an environmentally traumatized world: Healing ourselves and our planet* (pp. 113–140). Santa Barbara, CA: Praeger.

Marshall, B. (2016). 'No good news' for Louisiana: New study finds warming climate will lead to more frequent, intense storms. *The Advocate*, p. 4A.

Nemeth, D. G., Ray, K. P., & Schexnayder, M. M. (2003). *Helping your angry child: Worksheets, fun puzzles, and engaging games to help you communicate better.* Oakland, CA: New Harbinger Publications, Inc.

CHAPTER 5

Environmental Resilience

Abstract

This chapter discusses environmental resilience, with examples of issues to be addressed after an environmentally traumatic event. Significant examples of these issues include water pollution, damage to flood mitigation systems, erosion and depletion of wildlife habitats. Louisiana is considered to be a high-risk state environmentally, in need of intense remediation and conservation measures. Future housing development plans, repair and replacement of levees and dams, and other barriers to flooding and erosion are addressed with some reference to climate change. The text includes ways in which striking a balance between maximizing land use and protection of the ecosystem can be achieved.

Keywords: Environmental resilience; oikophilia; holistic planning; ecosystem

Contents

Louisiana could be the poster child for environmental trauma. According to Keim and Muller (2009), the State of Louisiana has experienced more environmentally traumatic events than any other state in the lower 48. Floods, hurricanes, tornados, coastal land loss, swamp degradation by oil companies, etc. You name it... we have experienced it! In spite of

Innovative Approaches to Individual and Community Resilience
DOI: http://dx.doi.org/10.1016/B978-0-12-803851-2.00005-2

nature-caused trauma, human-caused trauma, or both, Louisiana's environment has been amazingly resilient.

For example, after Hurricane Katrina, Lake Pontchartrain became excessively polluted by water from the New Orleans sewer system. Researchers from the US Geological Survey National Wetlands Research Center found that the lake's amoeba was able to successfully clear this up and return the lake to its pre-Katrina status. These findings were totally unexpected, but the lake took care of itself (Heitmuller & Perez, 2007). With humans' interference, however, this self-stabilization is becoming less likely.

IDEOLOGY AS FACT

Climate Change Denial, as an ideology, is ever-present (Dunlap & McCright, 2011). It is a belief, not a fact. In the most recent report issued by the Intergovernmental Panel on Climate Change (IPCC), the evidence is irrefutable. As the IPCC states, "Human influence on the climate system is clear, and recent anthropogenic emissions of greenhouse gases are the highest in history" (Pachauri & Meyer, 2014, p. 2), which have led to unprecedented changes over the past several decades in comparison to previous millennia. Most scientists are arguably quite attuned to the fact of climate change being exacerbated by human activity, which has caused a warming of the atmosphere and oceans, a decrease in the amount of snow and ice on the Earth's surface, and rising sea levels (Pachauri & Meyer, 2014).

RAINS AND FLOODS

After the Great Flood of 2016 in Louisiana, the National Oceanic and Atmospheric Administration issued a September 7, 2016 report titled "Climate Change increased chances of record rains in Louisiana by at least 40 percent." In this report, Karen van der Wiel explained, "We found human-caused heat trapping greenhouse gases can play a measurable role in events such as the August rains that resulted in such devastating floods affecting so many people." How many? "As of August 17, 2016, Louisiana officials reported that the flood had claimed 13 lives, more than 30,000 people had been rescued, more than 8,100 slept in shelters, and more than 60,000 homes had been damaged." Furthermore, the risk of similar events was expected to increase (National Oceanic and Atmospheric Administration, 2016).

TORNADOS

Earlier in 2016, Louisiana was hit by a wave of severe tornados wiping out homes and businesses. No loss of life, however, occurred.

One woman, who had just opened her new fitness business, offered the following: "We're all good. We're all safe and that's all that matters right now. This is a challenge for us but it's not going to stop us. We're going to put it back together and rebuild it better" (Goldman, 2016). The woman's gym had succumbed to a deadly tornado that ripped through Prairieville, Louisiana, and the surrounding areas. Like many structures in the tornado's path, the roof of the gym had been torn off. Sadly, this is the case for many buildings and homes that are impacted by devastating environmental trauma in Louisiana.

HURRICANES

Although there were no serious hurricane threats to Louisiana in 2016, this was quite unusual. Louisiana was spared, but Haiti was hit hard by Hurricane Matthew. In fact, 80% of the crops in some areas of the Island Nation was destroyed, in areas responsible for feeding 20,000 families (Ahmed, 2016). In spite of this, the Haitian children sent handmade pillows to Louisiana children who were affected by the Great Flood, with messages and artwork encouraging them to persevere. This was all a part of Dr. Judy Kurianksy's Global Kids Project. Dealing with nature-induced environmental trauma is bad enough, but when it is either human-caused or human-exacerbated, like in Hurricane Katrina, that is adding insult to injury (Landsea, 2011).

ENVIRONMENTAL INJURY

When one views aerial photographs of the many channels cut through the Louisiana wetlands, typically for the convenience of the oil companies, an eerie feeling of abuse and misuse arises. How can these wetlands survive when they have been so butchered for human use and consumption? Likewise, each manmade levee prevents the land from being restored (Marshall, 2017). All that wonderful run-off sediment is typically dumped off of the continental shelf by the Mississippi River. A March 2017 article in *The Advocate* stated "A main culprit, most agree is the river's levee system. Those bulwarks protect hundreds of thousands of people from regular inundation, but they also funnel millions of tons of sediment out of the mouth of the river into the Gulf, preventing that sand, clay, and organic matter from replenishing coastal lands, which are sinking due to a natural process known as subsidence"(Roberts, 2017). Again, little help is available for the wetlands, making coastal erosion and loss so much greater.

We need levees, but we also need a coastline. According to S. Jeffress Williams, senior scientist emeritus and research marine geologist of the US Geological Survey, it is estimated that 75 square kilometers of Louisiana coastline is lost every year (USGS, n.d.). Surely, with all of our human initiative and intelligence, there must be a way to prevent this loss.

Efforts to resolve this issue are being considered. A Mid–Barataria sediment diversion plan has been devised to alleviate the damage caused by the levee systems (Roberts, 2017). According to Faimon Roberts of *The Advocate*, "Under current plans, a hole will be cut in the levee there and replaced with a gated structure that could allow as much as 75,000 cubic feet per second of water and its accompanying sediment to flow down a channel and into the Barataria basin. But it wouldn't have to: The gates would allow operators to control the amount of water that flows into the basin" (2017, para. 8).

Natalie Peyronin, director of science policy at the Environmental Defense Fund states, "Our objective was always to maximize the land that we build or sustain but understanding that there has to be this balance between that and what the ecosystem needs are" (Roberts, 2017, para. 26).

DROUGHTS

Shortly after the August 2016 Great Flood, Louisiana farmers experienced many days of drought caused from fluctuations between too much and too little rain. Where is the balance? Why cannot the excessive rain water be preserved for the drought days? Again, there has got to be a way to do this. Reportedly, this growing imbalance has been predicted by climate change researchers (Marshall, 2016).

REACTION VERSUS PROACTION

Rather than waiting for a problem to occur, then jumping into action to handle it, perhaps creative planning to prevent what can be prevented and to manage what cannot be prevented might be a better course of action.

This would necessitate holistic cooperation involving moving away from the various silos of power and into a system that values integration of information. It would also require a shift away from humans perceiving themselves as conquerors of the land to being conservators of the land.

Although perception is not necessarily fact, it is the basis of human action (Nemeth & Olivier, 2015). When we perceive ourselves as owners of the land, we believe that it is ours to do with as we wish. This issue of entitlement has long been the basis of much abuse. When we perceive ourselves as caretakers of the land, however, we believe that it is ours to enjoy, but preserve, for future generations. But how?

As stated on the back of a return envelope of a 2016 National Geographic survey, "You may not be able to save the whole world, but you can make a difference in your own backyard by planting a garden of native plants to provide a sustainable habitat for local pollinators and other wildlife." We could recycle more. We could walk more and drive less. We could bring our own reusable grocery bags to the grocery store. We could keep reusable dishware in our offices instead of opting for one-time use plates and utensils. We could refill a glass water bottle rather than consuming water from a plastic water bottle. There are many small changes that we could make on a daily basis that could impact our environment, our home, for the better. Basically, all of us can do something! Think of the monumental impact even one small daily change by each of the seven billion people on this planet could make.

FROM MACRO MANAGEMENT TO MICRO MANAGEMENT

Although holistic planning may not be readily achievable, individual efforts to protect and preserve our environment *are* achievable. First, however, we must change our view of entitlement.

Native Americans got it right. But look at what happened to these altruistic people. They were, and still are, being crushed by entitled conquerors at every step along the way. In Louisiana, the Native Americans of Grand Bayou are fighting to preserve their wetlands (Marshall, 2016). As Rosina Phillipe, elder and spokeswoman for the Atakapas-Ishak/Chawaska Tribe stated, "For us, home is more than the building you live in. It's everything in the environment that surrounds you. If you leave, you become someone else. You are no longer the same person—no longer the same people." This statement was made in response to a 2007 Louisiana Coastal Restoration Plan that did not include consideration of this small coastal community in its proposal. Reportedly, because the people in this community were considered a "high risk," they were encouraged to move. But when you move, as Ms. Phillipe described, you lose your identity (Marshall, 2016).

A "HIGH-RISK" STATE

Louisiana is a "high-risk" state. Between the rains, the hurricanes, the tornados, active faults that produce structural damage (History McCulloh, 2001), and structural damage that is produced by inappropriate drilling (e.g., Lake Peigneur and Bayou Corne; Crowley & Pastrana, 2015), where can we move? Where should we go? How can we as a diverse, multicultural society give up our identity? The longing for our oikophilia is just too great. Relocating a community has been shamelessly tried in the past when the Cherokee people were forced out of the Carolinas and relocated to Oklahoma (History Channel, 2009), in the Trail of Tears that is now infamous in our American history.

Relocation of entire communities often does not work. Too much is lost in the process. Identities are destroyed. How can you put Humpty-Dumpty back together again? How can a glass that is shattered into a thousand pieces be repaired? This is not the solution, yet native habitats are constantly being threatened.

Another recent environmental threat has been the Dakota Access Pipeline, which was scheduled to run right through Sioux land and water resources (Yan, 2016). The Sioux people did not give permission for this, yet various industries believed they were entitled to continue on with the project. Only with the intervention of former President Barack Obama was bloodshed averted. The Sioux people, joined by many others, were prepared, in zero degree weather, to stand their ground. They were prepared to die to protect their environment. What are we prepared to do? Could we, at the very least, commit to making one small sustainable change in our daily lives?

FINDING SOLUTIONS AND COMPROMISES

Was it really that hard to find a way around the Sioux's water supply? Would it really be that hard to include the Grand Bayou Village Native Community in Louisiana's Coastal Restoration plans? Why do we need all those canals for the convenience of the oil companies? Convenience comes at a cost.

According to Bob Marshall's article in *The Advocate*, "Studies estimate the canals are responsible for up to 60 percent of the nearly 2,000 square miles of coastal wetlands lost since the 1930s" (2016, para. 17). Again—this is all because of human entitlement. There is a law in Louisiana that states that companies must fix what they disrupt (Act 361, La. R.S. 49:214.21), but they seldom are held accountable for doing so. In general, many companies tend not to be good stewards of the land.

Even ExxonMobil, one of the largest companies in the United States, uses Baton Rouge's precious drinking water from its underground aquifers, rather than Mississippi River water, as other plants do. With this misuse of Baton Rouge's water supply, A. Hays Town, Jr., estimates that Baton Rouge will only have 25 years of fresh drinking water remaining (2013). Why does ExxonMobil persist in this endeavor when other major industries, such as the Dow Chemical Company, use river water? Money! Profit! Entitlement!

Ms. Phillipe explained the difference in perception between conservators and conquerors as follows, "We don't think of the land—the environment—the way you do" (Marshall, 2016, para. 20). She went on to say, "It is part of us, essential to our life way. We can't live without it. So when it is unhealthy or sick, so are we. And when you destroy it, you are destroying our way of life" (Marshall, 2016, para. 20–21).

If Mr. Town, Jr., is correct, will ExxonMobil have destroyed our life way in 25 years? Baton Rouge is so used to having excellent drinking water. Will we all be forced to use bottled or boiled water in 25 years—just merely due to one company's sense of entitlement?

ENTITLEMENT IS OUR ENEMY

Our entire way of life, as well as our way of life in the future, is being threatened by people's sense of entitlement today. As Ms. Phillipe stated, "We have participated in the process. . . but they don't really hear us" (Marshall, 2016, para. 51). She concluded by saying that the tribe longs for restoration. "What the tribe really wants is for the companies and government that destroyed their wetlands to rebuild them," she stated (Marshall, 2016, para. 55). Is this really too much to ask?

As Ann Rolfes, director of the New Orleans-based Louisiana Bucket Brigade stated, "We've let so much be destroyed, and it's just time to stop it" (Burgess, 2016, pp. 1A, 4A). The Bucket Brigade is opposing the proposed Bayou Bridge Pipeline across the historic wetlands in the Atchafalaya Basin.

In the past, companies that built pipelines across the Atchafalaya Basin have, according to Dean Wilson, Executive Director of the conservation group Atchafalaya Basinkeeper, left "spoil banks" ... areas that "go for miles through the swamp," thus disrupting the Basin's ecosystem and prevent that natural flow of water through the swamp (Burgess, 2016, pp. 1A, 4A). Wilson argues for a return to the wetlands state "with no spoil banks left behind." Again, another example of where the law requiring restoration has not been followed by entitled people and companies.

Although plans to prevent coastal erosion have been in effect for years, will these plans be enough to save Louisiana's shrinking coastline? According to Bob Marshall's January 4, 2017 article in *The Advocate*, the 2017 edition of Louisiana's Coastal Master Plan predicts a grim future. This shocking plan revealed that "even if everything works as planned, 2800 square miles of coast could still be lost in the next four decades." Even more devastating is that "27,000 buildings may need to be flood proofed, elevated or bought out. . ." (Marshall, 2017, para. 3). This means that restoration alone may not be enough to save the coast. Despite restoration efforts, the coastline will still be greatly impacted by man-made levees, oil and gas dredging, and the rising sea level due to global warming (Marshall, 2017). These findings highlight the dire need for the entitled to modify their behavior, in order to save Louisiana from ongoing environmental trauma.

SUCCESS VERSUS SAFETY

In a 2016 article in *The Advocate* on Risk Factors by Jeff Adelson, Steve Hardy, and David Mitchell, scientist Craig Colten is quoted as stating, "Most municipal officials want to see their communities grow. That's the basic standard of success—not safety." This standard must now change. The Great Flood of 2016 taught Louisiana residents that success does not equal safety and that safety is far more important than growth. Pictures reveal mile after mile of subdivision growth inundated by water—18 inches in some places, six to eight feet in others—all ruined families' American dream of home ownership. Many of these homes should never have been built.

People were confused by the shifting flood maps from the Federal Emergency Management Agency (FEMA). If their homes were built in areas that were declared by FEMA as at a lower risk of flooding, people could obtain a mortgage without flood insurance. But these maps shift. Over the years, the first author's family home, for example, was sometimes declared to be in the flood risk zone and sometimes not. So, we purchased flood insurance regardless of how the current maps were drawn. That was because the first author's husband, Donald, is an Environmental Geologist. Most people, however, did not have the benefit of this information readily at hand. The prevailing preflood attitude was, *If you don't need it, don't get it.* Now things are different. It is safety first, *if* you can afford to rebuild.

REBUILDING

Reportedly, only 32,000 of the approximately 90,000−100,000 homes that were damaged in the 2016 Great Flood are eligible for federal assistance (Mitchell, 2016). The current funding rules are quite strict, and the majority will not qualify. During our Emotional Resiliency workshops, several people shared that the FEMA forms were too complicated and the proofs required were too overwhelming, so they simply gave up trying to seek government assistance. Many of these homes, however, were built in areas that should not have been developed. On November 2, 2016, Governor John Bell Edwards stated, "'We're committed to resilient rebuilding, not the status quo ante'" (Boone, 2016, para. 3). Edwards, in his speech to the Louisiana Smart Growth Summit, stated, "We are going to rebuild and thrive like never before" (Boone, 2016, para. 4). This will require a perceptual shift from "successful" growth to "safe" growth. According to Pat Forbes, Executive Director of the Louisiana State Office of Community Development, this fourth-costliest flood disaster in US history should serve as "a wake-up call" (Boone, 2016, para. 6). Infrastructure projects must be planned to increase resiliency, said Harriet Tregoning, Deputy Assistant Secretary for the US Department of Housing and Urban Development's Community Planning and Development office. When quoting this statistic, Tregoning reported, "85 percent of U.S. counties and parishes have been a presidentially declared disaster area in the past five years." She concluded that "People can't overcome natural systems and bend them to their will" (Boone, 2016, para. 9).

NATURAL SYSTEMS WILL PREVAIL

Human efforts to bend natural systems to their will are the major causes of environmental disasters. Building in areas that flood, preventing the swamps and wetlands from naturally replenishing themselves, cutting channels and building pipelines through the marshes, may be seen by entitled people and companies as progress, as "success." But these actions are bound to fail. Homes in flood plains will eventually flood. Wetland channels will cause coastal erosion. Pipelines will eventually break. The environment will be traumatized. How much can any environment stand before it collapses? As Ms. Phillipe so adroitly stated, "When the environment is sick, so are we" (Marshall, 2016, para. 21).

SICK ENVIRONMENT = SICK PEOPLE

In Michigan, children are suffering lead poisoning due to lead pipes that are bringing water to their homes (CNN Library, 2017). This is happening in St. Joseph, Louisiana, as well (Ballard, 2016). Our infrastructure is in such great need of repair. We should not have to have whistle-blowers, who are usually so badly mistreated for their honesty, bring these facts to our attention. It should be obvious that we need safe drinking water, safe bridges and roads, and safe places to live.

Safety requires being good stewards of our environment. When our environment is well, we are well. When our environment is sick or misused, we the people will eventually pay the price. Those who are entitled and those who are in positions of power seldom pay the price for their misdeeds. It is the "ordinary" people who are left to suffer. Perhaps, as the National Geographic statement proclaims, we cannot save the world. But we can save our little piece of the world by believing in common sense facts and by taking appropriate personal action. When we learn to live with our environment, as so many Native Americans do, we can make a real difference. Do we wish to continue our conquest of our environment or will we truly become conservators of our precious world? Environmental resilience depends on our actions. The choice is ours.

REFERENCES

Adelson, J., Hardy, S., & Mitchell, D. (2016). See FEMA claims, money distributed in your Baton Rouge are neighborhood after August flood. *The Advocate*, pp. 1A, 4A.

Ahmed, A. (2016). Hurricane Matthew makes old problems worse for Haitians. *The New York Times*. Retrieved from http://www.nytimes.com.

Ballard, M. (2016). Lead found in Saint Joseph drinking water in 20-plus percent of homes, businesses. *The Advocate*. Retrieved from http://www.theadvocate.com.

Boone, T. (2016). Floods highlight need to build smartly. *The Advocate*. Retrieved from http://www.theadvocate.com.

Burgess, R. (2016). Louisiana environmentalist mounting fight against proposed pipeline through the Atchafalaya Basin. *The Advocate*, pp. 1A, 4A.

CNN Library. (2017). Flint water crisis fast facts. *CNN*. Retrieved from http://www.cnn.com.

Crowley, N. & Pastrana, Jr., F. (2015). Grassroots leadership and involvement: Experiences and guidelines. In D.G. Nemeth & J. Kuriansky (Eds.), *Ecopsychology: Advances from the intersection of psychology and environmental protection* (pp. 35-52). Santa Barbara, CA: Praeger.

Dunlap, R. E., & McCright, A. M. (2011). Organized climate change denial. In J. S. Dryzek, R. B. Norgaard, & D. Scholsberg (Eds.), *The Oxford handbook of climate change and society* (pp. 144–160). Oxford, England: Oxford University Press. Available from http://dx.doi.org/10.1093/oxfordhb/9780199566600.003.0010.

Goldman, S. (2016). Tornado rips off roof, wall of Louisiana Gold's Gym. *iClubs*. Retrieved from http://www.iclubs.com.

Hays Town, Jr., A. (2013). A case history of use and management of the Baton Rouge fresh water aquifer system (Master's thesis). Louisiana State University, Baton Rouge, LA. Retrieved from http://etd.lsu.edu/docs/available/etd-04102013-180926/unrestricted/town_thesis.pdf.

Heitmuller, T., & Perez, B. C. (2007). Environmental impact of Hurricane Katrina on Lake Ponchartrain. In G. S. Farris, G. J. Smith, M. P. Crane, C. R. Demas, & L. L. Robbins (Eds.), *Science and the storms: The USGS response to the hurricanes of 2005* (pp. 231–238).

History Channel. (2009). *Trail of tears*. Retrieved from http://www.history.com.

Keim, B. D., & Muller, R. A. (2009). *Hurricanes of the Gulf of Mexico*. Baton Rouge, LA: LSU Press.

Landsea, C. W. (2011). Hurricanes and global warming. Retrieved online from the *National Oceanic and Atmospheric Administration's Atlantic Oceanographic and Meteorological Laboratory* website http://www.aoml.noaa.gov.

Marshall, B. (2016). "High risk" Native American village on Grand Bayou wants government help to stay as land disappears. *The New Orleans Advocate*. Retrieved from http://www.theadvocate.com/new_orleans.

Marshall, B. (2017). 2017 Coastal Master Plan predicts grimmer future for Louisiana coast as worst-case scenario becomes best-case. *The Advocate*. Retrieved from http://www.theadvocate.com/new_orleans.

McCulloh, R. P. (2001). Active faults in East Baton Rouge Parish, Louisiana. *Louisiana Geological Survey: Public Information Series No. 8*, 1–6. Retrieved from http://www.lgs.lsu.edu/deploy/uploads/8faults.pdf.

Mitchell, D. J. (2016). In first round flood money, East Rouge to get large share, but it won't go far. *The Advocate*. Retrieved from http://www.theadvocate.com.

National Oceanic and Atmospheric Administration. (2016). Climate change increased chances of record rains in Louisiana by at least 40 percent. *NOAA*. Retrieved from http://www.noaa.gov.

Nemeth, D. G., & Olivier, T. W. (2015). Perceptions of our environment. In D. G. Nemeth, & R. B. Hamilton (Eds.), *Ecopsychology: Advances from the intersection of psychology and environmental protection* (pp. 193–218). Santa Barbara, CA: Praeger.

Pachauri, R. K., & Meyer, L. A. (2014). Climate change 2014: Synthesis report. *Contribution of Working Groups I, II and III to the fifth assessment report of the Intergovernmental Panel on Climate Change (IPCC)*. Retrieved from the IPCC website http://www.ipcc.ch/report/ar5/wg2/.

Roberts, F. (2017). Wanted: Designs for transformational sediment diversion project for Mississippi River in Louisiana. *The Advocate*. Retrieved from http://www.theadvocate.com.

USGS (n.d.). Louisiana coastal wetlands: A resource at risk: USGS fact sheet. *USGS Coastal & Marine Geology Program*. Retrieved from https://pubs.usgs.gov/fs/la-wetlands

Yan, H. (2016). Dakota access pipeline: What's at stake? *CNN*. Retrieved from http://www.cnn.com.

CHAPTER 6

Achieving and Maintaining Individual Resilience

Abstract

This chapter continues the discussion of achieving and maintaining resilience, with emphasis on the psychosocial developmental aspects of resilience. The role of the family, which is integral to psychosocial development, is described as key to an environment where resilience can develop and thrive. The Hendrix developmental stages, and the resilience challenges at each stage, are explained and shown accompanied by the RILEE family affective themes.

A section on the role of spirituality is provided, underscoring the part it plays in a deeply religious locale such as Louisiana. The chapter is summarized with an example of a negative trait induced by trauma for each developmental stage.

Keywords: Psychosocial development; family; Hendrix developmental stages; spirituality; trauma

Contents

Innovative Approaches to Individual and Community Resilience
DOI: http://dx.doi.org/10.1016/B978-0-12-803851-2.00006-4

Louisiana's environment and its people have been amazingly resilient. But, how is this level of resilience achieved and maintained? In previous chapters, we have explored the biological underpinnings of resilience. In this chapter, we will focus primarily on the psychosocial developmental aspects of resilience.

Recent weather events in Louisiana, such as the Great Flood of August 2016 and the tornados of February 2017, have highlighted people's strong need for preserving their home, their "oikophilia," and their determination to persevere. In regard to the recent tornadoes, Livingston Parish President Layton Ricks stated, "It's been very disheartening and upsetting. Livingston Parish was overwhelmingly hit with the flood waters, but the people here are very resilient and we will all do all we can to help. We will all pitch in and get through this, but how many punches can we take?" (Toohey, 2017).

According to Frank Revitte, meteorologist at the National Weather Service's Slidell, Louisiana station, these were Enhanced Fujita-scale 3 (EF-3) tornados with maximum wind speeds of approximately 140 miles per hour. Nevertheless, there were no fatalities, which, as state climatologist, Barry Keim, remarked, was "the silver lining in something like this" (Toohey, 2017).

All in all, seven tornados touched down causing damage or destruction to over 700 homes in five Louisiana parishes. A state of emergency declared by Governor John Bel Edwards allowed federal recovery assistance (Toohey, 2017). Many areas, like Watson, LA, had not fully recovered from the August 2016 flood, or like New Orleans East, had still not recovered from Hurricane Katrina, which devastated that community over 10 years ago.

WHY STAY?

Over 80% of people born in Louisiana stay in Louisiana (Lane, 2014). Family ties are very strong in Louisiana, as is the culture. In November 2015, we were invited to conduct a Hurricane Katrina 10th Anniversary Workshop in the Lower 9th Ward of New Orleans. Although much of the community remained in shambles, people stayed. One woman lived in the only house that remained standing on her block. She shared that this was the first community event that she had attended since Katrina. She arrived after the workshop started and, at first, was a reluctant participant. With empathy and encouragement, however, she began to share.

She spoke of the loneliness and fear that she had experienced over the years. Another participant lost three children in Katrina. He had never spoken about this, containing his grief and suffering in silence. Yet, he felt safe enough to share and connect. That is what community is all about—an opportunity to share in safety.

When neighbors help neighbors and families remain strong, people stay and "get through this" (Toohey, 2017).

PSYCHOSOCIAL DEVELOPMENT

The role of the family is integral to psychosocial development. Most children are born into a family structure. In our book *Helping Your Angry Child*, coauthored with Kelly Paulk Ray and Maydel Morin Schexnayder (2003), we define "family" as the people who live in your household. Children look to these individuals for guidance, direction, and modeling of appropriate behaviors. In healthy environments, these children learn, grow, and flourish. They survive and thrive. They become resilient adults who can handle life's punches. No matter how smooth their childhood, life always includes punches. For example, according to Rehm (2015), 90% of people in the world experience some sort of trauma during their lifetime.

Experiencing trauma is now the "new normal." It is the rule, not the exception. What keeps people functioning can be traced back to their developmental experiences.

Those children who have experienced considerable developmental trauma do not fare as well. If they survive, they struggle to do so and certainly have a much more difficult time learning how to thrive, for they have not learned to be resilient.

There are resiliency challenges at each developmental stage in life. In order to highlight these challenges, we will use the following theories: Hendrix's Developmental Theory (1992), Murphy's Theory of Family Dysfunction (2001), and RILEE's Theory of Relating (Nemeth et al., 2003). These concepts may be found in the work of Nemeth et al. (2003) and are outlined in Tables 6.1−6.5. Each stage and corresponding dynamics will be discussed below.

STAGE 1: ATTACHMENT

According to Hendrix, this stage starts at birth and is typically completed by age 18 months (1992). During this stage of development, being

Table 6.1 Hendrix developmental theory and RILEE theory of relating

	Hendrix stages and ages	RILEE emotional needs	RILEE corrective behaviors
1	Attachment (0−18 months)	Attachment security	Relax
2	Exploration (18−36 months)	Attention	Relate
3	Identity (3−4 years)	Acceptance	Forgive
4	Competence (4−7 years)	Approval	Share
5	Concern (7−13 years)	Acknowledgment	Connect
6	Intimacy (13−19 years)	Affection	Satiate

Table 6.2 Hendrix/RILEE developmental theories

	Hendrix stages and ages	RILEE emotional needs	Hendrix messages	RILEE behaviors
1	Attachment (0−18 months)	Attachment security	I have a right to exist/be here	Being heard
2	Exploration (18−36 months)	Attention	I see the world as wonderful and exciting	Being positive
3	Identity (3−4 years)	Acceptance	This is me (who I am) world	Being understood
4	Competence (4−7 years)	Approval	I can do it (succeed)	Being successful
5	Concern (7−13 years)	Acknowledgment	I belong here	Being considered
6	Intimacy (13−19 years)	Affection	I can be close and loving	Being related

securely attached to mother or the primary caregiver is crucial. It allows the baby to relax. The Hendrix message to the baby is "you have a right to exist/to be here" (1992). When this message is disturbed or is not communicated, babies become scared, families become frantic, and tension ensues. Rather than experiencing comfort, babies experience distress. Oftentimes, they may react with manipulative behaviors in order to be heard. Then, in response, adults typically engage in either clinging or avoidant strategies, and stress becomes the predominant emotion in the family.

Table 6.3 RILEE/Murphy family dysfunction

	Family maladaptations	Hendrix's parental dynamics	Role of anger	Angry behaviors
1	Frantic	Clinging vs Avoiding	Stress	Create tension
2	Angry	Pursuing vs Isolating	Power	Control others
3	Troubled	Controlling vs Diffusing	Pain	Say mean things
4	Defective	Competing vs Manipulating	Embarrassment	Yell
5	Lonely	Caretaking vs Comforting	Sadness	Slap, kick, punch
6	Indulgent	Rebelling vs Conforming	Desire	Criticize, be dissatisfied

Table 6.4 RILEE method of being heard not hurt

	Breakdowns in caring	Hurt outcomes	RILEE resolutions	Healthy choices
1	Abandon	Manipulate	Create comfort	Commit
2	Intimidate	Isolate	Be friendly	Connect
3	Reject	Love conditionally	Create calmness	Love unconditionally
4	Abuse	React	Instill pride	Be proactive
5	Neglect	Control	Invite inclusion	Power
6	Betray	Mistrust	Listen actively	Trust

Table 6.5 Hendrix developmental stages and RILEE affective themes

Hendrix stages and ages	RILEE Core Fears	RILEE family affective themes
(1) Attachment (0–18 months)	Abandonment	Scared
(2) Exploration (18–20 months)	Loss	Angry
(3) Identity (3–4 years)	Shame	Anxious
(4) Competence (4–7 years)	Failure	Embarrassed
(5) Concern (7–13 years)	Being Alone	Sad
(6) Intimacy (13–19 years)	Losing Control	Happy/excessive desire

STAGE 2: EXPLORATION

This Hendrix stage typically lasts from age 18 to 36 months (1992). During this stage children are in constant need of attention. They explore. They are curious. They tend to "see the world as wonderful and exciting." They want to relate. When this desire is positively reinforced, children begin to connect to the world around them. When it is not or it is negatively reinforced, children become angry. They throw temper tantrums. They try to control others via powerful intimidations. These behaviors are designed to avoid isolation and a sense of loss. These children are trying to connect, but in unhealthy ways. They do not know any better. They are merely modeling their caretakers who are either exhibiting pursuing or isolating behaviors. Such behaviors do not work. Therefore, children learn maladaptive ways of coping. Rather than learning to survive and thrive, the essence of resilience, they are learning to create drama and chaos.

STAGE 3: IDENTITY

This important developmental task, according to Hendrix, usually takes place between ages 3 and 4 (1992). Children are coming to grips with who they are. The Hendrix message, "this is me (who I am) world," is a very powerful one (1992). Children learn to accept themselves and all of their defining characteristics (e.g., race, gender, language). With self and/or other acceptance "as is," children feel understood. This is the basis for the development of self-esteem.

When a child's identity is denied or is considered to be "not okay," then feelings of shame and/or anxiety set in. This causes considerable emotional pain for the child, both inside and outside of the family unit. Children may respond by saying mean things to either themselves or others. The concept of "I'm not okay" begins to set in. Shame reigns. Children become troubled, and adult caregivers respond by either trying to control or diffuse their child's pain. Rejection ensues. Love becomes conditional. Children do not feel understood, let alone accepted for who they really are. Forgiving the pain and creating calmness may not ensue, especially if the child is not the "hoped for" child. If children are "different," they then begin to expect rejection from the world. These children are not resilient. They are troubled and they expect trouble from others. They frequently are on "red alert." Because of their perceived lack of acceptance, it is very hard for these children to be a part of a team. Instead, they lash out in pain. This tends to carry through into adulthood.

STAGE 4: COMPETENCE

It is every child's dream to become competent, to succeed, and to be good at something. In fact, Hendrix's developmental message is "you can do it (succeed)" (1992). When children receive this message from their caregivers, they internalize it. They survive and thrive. They become the little engines that could. They achieve resilience. This proactive message, this sense of approval is usually conveyed to children, according to Hendrix, between ages 4 and 7 (1992). Children are taught that they can be successful. Pride is instilled, and children blossom. When children get the message from their caregivers or others that they are defective, problems ensue. If a child is dyslexic or has a medical condition, such as spina bifida, caregivers may feel embarrassed. These children then begin to introject the parental message of failure. Once children begin to perceive themselves as defective, maladaptive coping strategies ensue. Oftentimes considerable yelling becomes a part of the family structure, and the parent figures become increasingly manipulative or competitive toward one another or their environment. In school, for example, these parents may have unrealistic expectations of teachers regarding their ability to solve their children's problems. They may also exhaustively seek help from a variety of professionals to resolve these unresolvable problems. Many problems, such as intellectual disabilities, are persistent, however, thus trapping parents into being forever caretakers. These children are unable to survive and thrive in that environment. Yet, some problems, even those that were previously deemed incurable (e.g., many forms of childhood cancer), can be resolved with the right intervention. When a problem is proactively addressed and resolved, those children can survive and thrive. In fact, they can lead the way. When problems cannot be resolved, adaptations must be made.

STAGE 5: CONCERN

From ages 7 to 13, children enter the age of concern (Hendrix, 1992). That is when the need for belonging is paramount. As Hendrix points out, the developmental message of "I belong here" really sets in. For children in this age group, this message is usually tested in school. Children must be able to connect to their peers. They must be acknowledged and affirmed. Fitting in, so to speak, is crucial. Every child needs friends—a peer group to offer inclusion. Inclusion is so powerful at this stage. Without inclusion, children feel sad and alone. They do not feel powerful. Instead, they feel unwanted. This dynamic may also be happening on the home front where parental figures may be trying to either comfort or caretake. But, even parents may not be able to make up for their children's ostracization. When parent figures become overwhelmed with this task, they may begin to withdraw affection and even further add to their children's sense of isolation or loneliness. These sad children may respond by acting out, by slapping, kicking, or punching others. By having no one to whom they can connect, these children may resort to violence as a way of expressing their frustration. Rather than lashing out, however, these children need to learn the power of recognizing, labeling, and sharing their feelings. As adults, those who lash out are not truly powerful or respected. They act without thinking, create problematic situations, and exacerbate already difficult situations.

STAGE 6: INTIMACY

Ah, adolescence! Some say that God made adolescence so that we will more easily learn how to let go of our children. Yet, the developmental task of adolescence is to give children both roots and wings. The roots come from helping children successfully locomote the first five developmental stages. But the sixth stage is the most demanding of all. This is the stage in which parents must help their children to develop wings and to learn how to fly. In spite of their effort to create separation from their parent figures, adolescents must learn, according to Hendrix, that they "can be close and loving" without feeling smothered (1992). This is quite a challenge. Appropriate ways of relating and satiating must be modeled. Learning when to say *when*, so to speak, is essential. How much affection is too much? How much is too little? Setting and respecting boundaries is crucial. When adolescents lose control and over-indulge, things turn out badly. Whether it is alcohol or drugs or sex or the Internet, any addiction as a result of poor boundaries and/or excessive desire prevents adolescents from surviving and thriving. They fail to launch into adulthood and fail to achieve their rightful place in society. They are more than rebellious, for all adolescents become rebellious at times; rather, they become critical of and dissatisfied with life. Direct and/or indirect forms of suicide may be ultimate expressions of their sense of mistrust in and feelings of betrayal by the world. Whether rebelling or conforming, these overly indulgent adolescents become a plague on society and often end up in jail, in addiction treatment programs, or both. Their entry into adulthood has been thwarted by over-indulgence, and they have not learned to fly.

Most adolescents, however, do not succumb to these temptations. They remain related to their parents and find happiness in spite of the myriad of developmental problems that confront them. They seek affection, affiliation, success, and happiness. They find ways to survive and thrive. These adolescents are able to take their rightful place in adult society. They contribute. They survive. They thrive. For they are the resilient ones.

MAINTAINING RESILIENCE

Once individuals have successfully locomoted the Six Stages of Development (Hendrix, 1992), they have learned to create comfort, be friendly, create calmness, instill pride, invite inclusiveness, and listen actively. These behaviors have been modeled by their parents/caregivers. They have also learned to understand their own emotional needs for attachment security, attention, acceptance, approval, acknowledgment, and affection. They understand that they must make healthy choices, even when life throws them a punch, or several punches. They must choose to make commitments, to connect to others, to love unconditionally, to be proactive, to seek power and control over themselves and their behavior, and to trust in others so that workable goals can be achieved. As Layton Ricks said in response to the tornadoes that touched down in Watson, LA, "We will all pitch in and get through this" (Toohey, 2017). He added, however, ". . . But how many punches can we take?" (Toohey, 2017).

Resilient people can take as many punches as needed. Feeling scared, angry, anxious, embarrassed, sad, and even happy are all temporary feelings that resilient people experience post-environmental trauma. After the tornados touched down on February 2, 2017, so many commented that they were just happy to be alive.

REGRESSION IN SERVICE OF THE EGO

When a disaster happens, we each regress developmentally and revisit the developmental stages outlined above. Frequently, it is a quick trip down memory lane wherein we remind ourselves that we can, once again, survive and thrive for we are the resilient ones. We remind ourselves of the developmental messages that we received: that we have a right to exist and be here; that our world is a wonderful place; that we are loveable, capable, and valuable; that we can regroup and rebuild; that we belong here, that this is our "oikophilia"; and that we can continue to be a close and loving family in spite of it all.

This is what resilience is all about. No matter what happens, no matter what fate brings our way, we will persevere. We have learned to do this and we will prevail.

THE ROLE OF SPIRITUALITY

After the Great Flood of August 2016, a cartoon appeared in *The Advocate* (Fig. 6.1). It read, "I didn't know Noah was a Cajun." This cartoon appeared in response to "The Cajun Navy," a unique example of neighbor helping neighbor, Louisiana style. As was true in response to Hurricane Katrina, many people who had fishing boats came to the aid

Figure 6.1 Noah's Cajun Navy.

of stranded families, often on rooftops, who were flooded out. No one told them to come; they just did. As a result, only 13 people lost their lives in the flood. People came from all over the State with their small boats to rescue others. They just did the right thing. They were there before any official agency could respond. They were the "Noahs" of Louisiana.

It is not by chance that these people were called "Noahs," for Louisiana is a deeply religious state. In Louisiana, religion and psychology go hand-in-hand to help people. After the Great Flood and tornados, a State Agency from the Department of Health and Human Resources, called the Louisiana Spirit, went everywhere, to every household and shelter to help the people. They informed those who suffered of the availability of counseling and emotional support.

These counselors, who were flooded themselves, participated in the Louisiana Psychological Association's Emotional Resiliency Workshops for adults, children, and teens. These workshops, just as in Hurricane Katrina's first and 10th anniversary workshops, were held in churches. In the South, the church is frequently the center of one's community. Therefore, church, state, and local psychological organizations work hand-in-hand to help people. During times of environmental trauma, people from many different backgrounds and beliefs work together to help one another. This integrated community response is an expression of solidarity and resilience. By being firmly present in today and by learning from yesterday, these community responses help all to see themselves in a better tomorrow. Goodwill prevails, and environmental trauma is overcome. Most thank God for their resilience. At the end of many of our workshops, "We Shall Overcome" (Jackson, 1993) was spontaneously sung to express participants' determination to persevere.

THE EFFECTS OF DEVELOPMENTAL TRAUMA ON RESILIENCY

Many were born with the biological propensity for resilience. Some were not quite so fortunate. As discussed in an earlier chapter, for the latter individuals, the development of posttraumatic stress disorder after a major and/or ongoing traumatic event is much higher.

If the traumatic event or series of events occur during child development, the results can be catastrophic.

To review, if trauma occurs during the ages of Attachment, chronic fear may result; during the ages of Exploration, chronic anger may be present; during the ages of Identity, chronic anxiety may occur; during the ages of Competence, a tendency toward being easily embarrassed may be present; during the ages of Concern, an underlying sadness may linger; and during the ages of Intimacy, a Pollyannaish happiness or excessive desire may be inappropriately present (Table 6.5).

Especially in Stage 6, this lack of satiation or excessive desire can lead to reckless behavior and/or addiction. Boundaries are important at every stage of development. Accepting one's limits leads to satisfaction and comfort. Not learning to do so may result in considerable dissatisfaction and distress. Then the unresolved issues from that developmental stage are expressed via the dominant emotional theme of that period: Stage 1—scared, Stage 2—angry, Stage 3—anxious, Stage 4—embarrassed, Stage 5—sad, or Stage 6—happy/excessive desire.

When these developmental issues remain unresolved in that particular stage, children are left with emotional scars. The following breakdowns in caring tend to be repeated throughout the years. For example, if in Stage 1, a child feels, senses, or experiences abandonment, that child is prone to be fearful. In Stage 2, if considerable intimidation was present, that child develops an angry adaptation. In Stage 3, if rejection was common, chronic anxiety results. In Stage 4, if abuse was present, the child is plagued with a sense of ongoing embarrassment. In Stage 5, if there was neglect, sadness is the adaptation. And in Stage 6, if the child, now an adolescent, felt betrayed, trust is lost and the inability to satiate becomes overwhelming. These children want to be heard, for someone to acknowledge and verify their pain; however, sadly they are often not heard.

For example, now at age 22, a young woman who was sexually victimized as an adolescent, chronically expresses her desire to be heard and her pain to be acknowledged by the appropriate authority figures. Sadly, defense and denial continue to be the responses she receives, even after all these years. She writes, "I wish I could say that I have the energy to keep up the good fight, but after eight years the soul begins to weaken, yet I am constantly reminded why resilience is important to survival" (personal correspondence used with permission of the author).

This young woman notes that "Life continues despite trying to recover from trauma. The flash of the camera hits you and at that moment it captures your eyes holding onto the tears that you were trying to hide, a smile that's fake, and the misery seeping out of your skin."

She then writes, "I couldn't get away from the trauma, I couldn't snap my fingers and be recovered or healed. I survived not by the day, but sometimes by the minute... the guilt I was consumed with overwhelmed me... I didn't quite understand why... I wanted to be a normal ninth grader, but being so depressed that doing normal 15-year-old things felt like an insult to my trauma... normal was a word that left my life. Nothing made sense... It was exhausting and painful... and some days lying to myself that I would be OK and that life would get better. Unfortunately, it would be years before anything would feel better or normal."

Eventually, this adolescent succumbed to the pressure of the trauma and began engaging in reckless and/or self-harming behaviors. Hospitalization was needed. Subsequent outpatient therapy and medication management eventually lead to satiation and stabilization. As she wrote, "I would not have crawled out of my depression hole," without these interventions. Her mantra changed from "get me through this minute" to "just keep looking up." Hope began to return. As she concluded, "If we can't face our trauma with truth, we will never recover. I chose recovery, but I went to sleep many nights wondering if rebuilding my life and perception was worth the pain."

She offered this advice, "I questioned how I survived... it was a choice, honestly, it may sound naïve to think of recovery like that, but it comes down to a simple choice of 'do I let this ruin me or do I endure to survive and be a better person?'" She chose to survive and thrive.

CHILDREN KNOW

Children may not have the words to express their pain, but they do know when something is wrong. They sense it. They feel it. And they respond with whatever behaviors are available to them. In Stage 1, their distress is displayed via crying and/or screaming. These behaviors create tension in the parents/caregivers who may respond with leaving the infant alone to cry, which is the exact opposite of what the infant needs. The infant wants to be swaddled, to be soothed, but instead is left alone. In Stage 2, the child may attempt to control the parents/caregivers through powerful displays. Instead of relating and modeling appropriate interactive behaviors, the tired parent/caregiver may just isolate from the child. This leaves the child feeling lost. In Stage 3, the child may say mean things to get attention; however, this may result in shaming. In Stage 4, the child may yell and scream to be heard but often fails to get the desired message across. This sense of failure to succeed and be heard can stay with a child for a long time, resulting in underperformance. In Stage 5, physical violence such as slapping, kicking, and/or punching may be present, especially among children whom others have failed to hear. These children are very lonely. They do not know how to connect. They are headed for trouble. In Stage 6, these adolescents become very critical, very rebellious. They criticize and are criticized in return. Dissatisfaction reigns. Trust is gone. Instead, they feel betrayed. They often lose control and choose unhealthy behaviors. These are the adolescents who have not been heard.

Whether infants or adolescents, children innately know when something is wrong, when their needs are not being met or their realities are not being acknowledged. They sense when they are a burden rather than a joy. Without appropriate intervention, these children become developmentally arrested. Then when something goes wrong in their adult life, they often do not have the resilience to handle it. Instead, they regress to that developmental stage in their life where they have unfinished business. They tend to cope with the reality of the present with the dysfunctional behaviors and emotions of the past. If in Stage 1, they may become very manipulative. If in Stage 2, they may isolate. If in Stage 3, everything becomes very conditional. If in Stage 4, they can be very reactive. If in Stage 5, they may present as very controlling. And if in Stage 6, they become very mistrustful.

REBUILDING RESILIENCY

When a traumatic event occurs and resilience appears to be lacking, it is important to understand regression. At times, people regress to earlier developmental stages in order to cope with whatever they are facing. Understanding the behaviors and emotions that are often displayed in each of these developmental stages allows for the rebuilding of resiliency. During our initial Katrina workshops, our 10-year Katrina anniversary workshops, and our post Great Flood workshops, these concepts were used to address developmental regression and rebuild resiliency. The Six Stages were explained, people identified their "go to" behaviors and emotions. When these emotions were recognized, labeled, and shared, they were, once again, able to be firmly grounded in the present. They were able to take a trip down memory lane and learn from, rather than remain in the past, so that they could see themselves recovering and rebuilding for a better tomorrow.

This fluidity in times of trauma is what is necessary to achieve and maintain resilience.

REFERENCES

Hendrix, H. (1992). *Keeping the love you find: A guide for singles*. New York: Simon & Schuster, Inc.

Jackson, M. (1993). We shall overcome [CD]. Charly.

Keim, B. D., & Muller, R. A. (2009). *Hurricanes of the Gulf of Mexico*. Baton Rouge, LA: Louisiana State University Press.

Lane, E. (2014). Louisiana has most native-born residents in the country, New York Times reports. *The Times Picayune*. Retrieved February 15, 2017, from < http://www.nola.com/politics/index.ssf/2014/08/louisiana_has_most_native-born.html >.

Murphy, T., & Oberlin, L. H. (2001). *The angry child: Regaining control when your child is out of control*. New York: Clarkson Potter Publishers.

Nemeth, D. G., Ray, K. P., & Schexnayder, M. M. (2003). *Helping your angry child*. Oakland, CA: New Harbinger.

Rehm, D. (2015). The science of resilience and how it can be learned [Audio blog post]. Retrieved February 13, 2017, from < http://dianerehm.org/shows/2015-08-24/the-science-of-resilience-and-how-it-can-be-learned >.

Toohey, G. (2017). Strong, rare EF-3 twister struck Watson on Tuesday, same classification as one that hit New Orleans East. *The Advocate*. Retrieved February 13, 2017, from < http://www.theadvocate.com/baton_rouge/news/article_9e0dcbbe-eeed-11e6-86ad-a30873fc446b.html >.

CHAPTER 7

Becoming a Resilient Clinician

Abstract

This chapter discusses the necessity of achieving and maintaining resilience in order to be a resilient clinician. Suggestions on how to resolve external and internal sources of conflict are made by the authors. Emphasis on a positive outlook and the ability to see oneself in tomorrow are keys in the definition of a grounded clinician.

Maintaining perspective, fostering healthy personal relationships, allowing time to learn from others, keeping ethical boundaries, and resolving past issues are some concepts that are emphasized in order to achieve success. Perspectives and insights from experienced professionals are provided. A list of references is included for supplemental information.

Keywords: Modeling; balance; healthy boundaries; self-care; memories; choices

Contents

Innovative Approaches to Individual and Community Resilience
DOI: http://dx.doi.org/10.1016/B978-0-12-803851-2.00007-6

As clinicians, we are entrusted with the most precious of packages—the lives of other individuals. Day in and day out, we find ourselves seated across from another, and we do our best to make positive impacts with the hope of effecting meaningful change. For many of us, this is exactly why we chose the field that we did—we want to *help people*. Do we, though, really understand what this means, and more important, do we know *what it costs?*

Becoming a clinician necessitates a tremendous amount of work and carries with it an incredible amount of responsibility. There are typically many years of study required to gain entry into the field of the helping professions. For some, especially those at the doctoral level, this could represent 9 years of study or more, extended time away from family and friends to attend school, several years of practicum, internship, and postdoctoral fellowship with wages that are often nonexistent or below the federal poverty level, plus debt resulting from student loans to pay for it all. Oftentimes, life activities typical of young adulthood, such as marriage, having children, and buying a home, are delayed in the process. During these years, we learn that *the patient comes first*, and we often put aside our own needs, feelings, and desires, to learn more, do more, and help more.

As one progresses, this way of thinking becomes second-nature, a new cognitive schema that influences the way we perceive ourselves, others, and the world around us. This schema is further reinforced upon the realization that people seek our help when they are in crisis—in general, no one comes to see us when things are going well. Although this may seem intuitive, the effects of such a profession are not immediately understood. "They need me, so I must always make myself available," we may think to ourselves. This is arguably even more relevant for new and early career professionals. People come to us in crisis—when they are at their lowest points, when they have just suffered a tremendous loss, when trauma knocks at their door, when they are faced with losing everything, when they have received a life-altering diagnosis, or when they finally recognize the devastating effects of an unhealthy lifestyle. With so many problems to address, taking care of oneself is usually not even close to being on the agenda.

SEASONING MAKES EVERYTHING BETTER

There is something magical about living in the South. Most important is the fact that our food just tastes better (the authors acknowledge their biases). If there is one thing that Southern cooks have mastered, it is the art of seasoning, and we are not just talking about salt and pepper! Undoubtedly, seasoning makes everything better, not just food. So what does seasoning have to do with learning to become a more resilient clinician?

Modeling is a bona fide behavioral concept that is widely used by therapists, teachers, and parents around the world. We believe that it is a concept that can also be very relevant for discussions regarding developing resilience. As such, it is imperative that we learn from others who have proven to be resilient throughout their lives—these are the *seasoned professionals*. This takes active effort on our parts—to seek out, discover, and take the time to understand what it takes to develop a greater level of resiliency in our own lives.

This chapter seeks to provide perspectives from some of these seasoned clinicians, as well as thoughts from an early career perspective, in an effort to reach out to our fellow colleagues and renew hope in a candid way.

REFLECTIONS FROM A SEASONED PROFESSIONAL

When I was about to take my 5-day, 40-hour doctoral exams, Don Glad, PhD, my mentor in Community Psychology told me, "Darlyne, if you don't know it by now, you won't learn it by cramming. Go get a manicure, have your hair done, sleep well, and come well-dressed each day to take the exams." I will never forget those wise words. I followed them to a tee and was one of only 3 out of the 11 candidates to pass.

Over the last 40+ years, I have continued to follow Don's advice. Pacing is a key to become one resilient clinician. Overworking and lack of self-care are not. I always remind myself of the directions from the airplane stewardess who tells us that, in the event of a problem and the oxygen masks are released, first put the mask on yourself, then help others.

APPEARANCES ARE IMPORTANT

A resilient clinician understands the wisdom of this statement. If you are not doing well, how can you help others? This is true both externally and internally. If you do not sleep well, eat well, dress well, etc., how can you model these behaviors for your patients? That does not mean that you have to look like a Victoria Secret or GQ model, but you must look presentable. Appearances count. How can you expect your patients to take care of themselves when you do not? Remember, however, not to overdress or overdo it.

The second author vividly recalls counting down the days remaining until the completion of the internship training year. One of my colleagues, Dr. Thea Norris, used to remind us each day that all that was required was that we "dress up and show up" (personal communication, 2016)—everything else would follow. I will never forget her words, for they were filled with veiled wisdom.

One must first be present to be resilient. Too often, people run from difficult experiences, missing out on valuable opportunities to grow—both professionally and personally. Just as a muscle grows by adding consistent, incremental weight, so, too, we grow by enduring through tough circumstances. We must learn to discern when to engage and when to withdraw. To be consistently present is a valuable skill. Having *all the answers* is not nearly as important as being present and available.

Second, how we present ourselves is of the utmost importance. In the South, we have a longstanding tradition of "dressing up." Mothers teach their daughters to be presentable upon leaving the house. This often includes appropriate clothing, makeup, *and* hair. Although seemingly insignificant and even petty to some, these traditions speak to the importance of putting one's best foot forward. When you "dress up and show up," you learn to persevere through challenging situations; when you show up *and* do so in a presentable manner, you start to develop the integrity that is needed to further build resilience. You become known as a trustworthy and responsible person.

BE ATTUNED TO YOUR INNER LIFE

Likewise, a resilient clinician must take care of his or her own internal life. Being overwhelmed by anxiety or depression is not acceptable; rather managing such feelings is the goal. Resilient clinicians pay attention to their inner life. They recognize, label, and address/resolve their feelings. They accept their humanity and expect to be overcome by normal feelings at stressful times (e.g., grief reactions). But they do not get stuck in these anxious or sad feelings. They deal with them.

Denial. Stoicism. Substance abuse. These are coping strategies that are maladaptive. Patients can sense when a clinician is not fully present. Maladaptive coping behaviors interfere with a clinician's effectiveness. How can a clinician sense how a patient is truly feeling when that clinician is not addressing his or her own true feelings? This may allow technical competence, but not emotional competence.

"THANKS, BUT NO THANKS"

Personal resources (e.g., time, energy, and money) are finite. This means that when resources are devoted to one thing, they are *not being devoted* to something else.

Years ago, the concept of multitasking became a hot topic in popular culture. People fell in love with the idea that it was possible to do more in less time. Productivity was idolized. *Busyness* became synonymous with *importance and worth*. Interestingly, research started to reveal some loopholes within the ideas of multitasking and busyness. Did our productivity actually increase as we became busier?

Adler and Benbunan-Fich (2012) described an inverted relationship between multitasking and productivity. Namely, if one is under stimulated, it can be difficult to focus due to low motivation. On the other hand, overstimulation can also damage alertness and attention, again leading to distraction. Consistent with previous literature, performance is maximized by balance. As Susanne M. Jensen, PhD, indicated, a lifestyle of balance, inclusive of rest and play, is an essential part of becoming a resilient clinician (2015).

In a day and age where we are constantly connected through smart phones, smart televisions, and a whole host of other smart devices, are we actually becoming more intelligent, more connected, more productive? In a review of the literature on smart phone usage, Kushlev, Proulx, and Dunn (2016) report that we check our phones over 100 times daily, using our phones at social events, while working, and even while we are having sex! Kushlev and colleagues conclude that cell phone interruptions (e.g., notifications) caused inattention and hyperactivity in the general population, stating that "being constantly interrupted by alerts and notifications may be contributing towards an increasingly problematic deficit of attention in our digitally connected society" (p. 9). Remember, resources are finite, and productivity is maximized by a sense of *balance,* not overproduction, overstimulation, and/or overworking.

So how can one maximize productivity while still maintaining a sense of balance and fostering resilience? In describing the magnificent beauty of a rosebush, Cloud (2010) notes that there is "a method behind the beauty" (p. 15). This method, known as *pruning,* is as applicable to the development of resilience as it is to the beautification of a flower garden. As Cloud states, "Pruning is a process of proactive endings. It turns out that a rosebush, like many other plants, cannot reach its full potential without a very systematic process or pruning" (p. 15). He explains that the skilled gardener "intentionally and purposefully" prunes branches that fall into one of three categories: "1. Healthy buds that are not the best ones, 2. Sick branches that are not going to get well, and 3. Dead branches that are taking up space needed for the healthy ones to thrive" (pp. 15–16).

Implementing a personal pruning process is essential to becoming more resilient. Life is expansive and creates more opportunities than an individual can seize. As such, we must carefully and wisely consider where, when, and how to most effectively allocate our resources. To do this, one must learn to say no just as often, if not more, than to say *yes.*

Pruning allows resources to be freed up for use in the tasks and activities that show the greatest potential (Cloud, 2010) and prevents overstimulation and over involvement, which can lead to distraction and ineffectiveness. The more distracted we become, the more stress we experience. The more stress we experience, the more frustrated and irritable we become. The more frustrated and irritable we become, the less resilient we become. The less resilient we become, the less effective we become. Therefore, learning the power of "thanks, but no thanks" is an important element of developing greater personal resilience.

REST

You are probably familiar with the common saying, "I'll rest when I die." Unfortunately, this statement has become a sad reality for many. Successful professionals often believe that the proper time for rest follows the completion of one's work. "Work before play" is drilled into us as children and reinforced in school. Nevertheless, as the world's pace continues to advance at an ever-increasing rate, we find ourselves with more and more on our schedules. Too often, our bodies force us to rest by invoking sickness because we simply will not stop. Busyness is synonymous with importance. In our minds, we reserve rest for the unsuccessful, less important, "not-smart-or-you-would-be-working-as-hard-as-me" people.

Wayne Muller, PhD, author of *Sabbath*, would beg to differ. In describing the irrefutable need for rest, he so eloquently explains, "When we breathe, we do not stop inhaling because we have taken in all the oxygen we will ever need, but because *we have all the oxygen we need for this breath*. Then we exhale, and make room for more oxygen. Sabbath [or, rest], like the breath, allows us to imagine we have done enough work *for this day*" (1999, p. 83).

Every physiological and biological process follows an unseen rhythm. Our bodies and our minds are no exception. We must learn to heed this rhythm and make room for rest in our lives.

DEFINING RESILIENCY

As stated in earlier chapters, we define resiliency as being firmly grounded in today, while benefitting from yesterday, so that we can see ourselves in tomorrow. Let us break that down.

TODAY

Are your relationships in order? Are you in order? What does this even mean? Let's start with you. Do you have an emotional balance? Do you understand how you are feeling? A wonderful clinician named Reuvan Bar-Levav, MD, wrote a book titled, *Thinking in the Shadow of Feelings* (1988). Basically in 366 pages, he said that it cannot be done. We agree. Being a resilient clinician requires the ability to be a very creative thinker who can facilitate effective problem solving in his/her patients. Unresolved emotions interfere with creative thinking and problem solving. Clinicians who are not emotionally balanced cannot be present to their patients. Basically, they are not in today. Being in today requires being fully present.

Oftentimes this lack of presence is due to conflict. Conflict in personal or professional relationships. Conflict in business experiences. Conflict in barriers that are created by managed care requirements. For example, as a practicing medical psychologist, the bane of the senior author's professional existence is the Prior Authorization Process. This is not used for the benefit of the patient, but rather for the benefit of the insurance company to control costs. Usually the less expensive drugs must be tried first, rather than those medications that are more likely to be effective for the patient. After doing my best to resolve this dilemma, I do share my frustration with my patient, for we are a team. We have a relationship. My patient is entitled to know how I feel about things that directly impact his or her care. Then, we strategize together. *Together* being the operative word.

You, as a resilient clinician, are not in this experience alone. You have a partner—your patient. Treatment is not something that you are doing to him or her, but rather *with* him or her. This is especially true when you have a patient with an illness that requires medication. For example, one of the most problematic situations is that of the Bipolar patients who will not stay on their medication regimen. Oftentimes, in a manic high, these patients believe that they do not need these medications to keep themselves balanced. My experience has been that, even with schizophrenic patients, a mutually trusting relationship, not a technique, will help them to save themselves from disaster. This is also true of patients in a severe depressive state. If they can perceive the clinician as their partner, not just their doctor, perhaps in returning from the brink of a depressive episode, suicide may be avoided.

Being a good clinical partner does not mean that any breaches of ethics, boundaries, and/or confidentiality have occurred. Rather, it means that patients perceive you as a balanced, caring entity who has the ability to share their journey with them. Somewhere deep inside themselves they know that they are not alone. Except for borderline personality disorders, who do not respect anyone's boundaries, patients will be amazingly respectful of a clinician whom they regard as resilient.

Part two of this lesson has to do with personal relationships. How can you, as a clinician, be effective when your own life is in shambles? This is not resilience. Life is not easy. Things go wrong. People die. They disappoint. Resilient clinicians understand the limits of their own resilience. When a child or a partner dies, grieving is expected. A clinician who is grieving can still be effective. The key, once again, is to recognize, label, and process or share your feelings. When needed, that is what support groups and/or psychotherapy can offer.

YESTERDAY

Memories are the cornerstones of our lives. They allow perspective. They encourage balance. They promote thoughtful action rather than emotional reaction. They can either be our best friends or our worst enemies. It is up to us how we use them. A resilient clinician uses his or her memories for guidance. Memories can be used to facilitate, rather than restrict, choices.

When we are afraid of our memories, when their places in our minds and hearts are unresolved, they become restrictive. When we have processed them into perspective, they become facilitative. As resilient clinicians, our responsibility is to learn from these memories so that they become assets in the present. No matter how painful the memories or how joyful, it is our responsibility to use them to enhance our choices.

TOMORROW

And then there is tomorrow. If we cannot see ourselves in tomorrow, we will not be there. We will be eternally stuck in the past with only regrets to guide us—to guide us to nowhere. That is how many of our patients fail themselves. But we, as resilient clinicians, must not get stuck there. We must always have something, some experience to look forward to in our future. These experiences, however, do not fall from the sky. We must create them. This requires being fully alive in our personal and professional lives. We must engage in professional activities like presenting at conferences, growth experiences like workshops or teaching/ mentoring, leadership experiences like becoming an officer in various clubs or organizations, traveling, reading, learning, etc. We cannot afford to be stagnant, to be satisfied with what we know. Healthy striving allows us to make a place for ourselves in the future.

For example, the senior author has recently completed two terms on the American Psychological Association's Council of Representatives (APA CoR) and the Louisiana Psychological Association's Executive Committee (LPA EC). In order not to stagnate, I have also accepted a position on the International Organizing Committee of the II Congress on Mental Health: Meeting the Needs of the XXI Century that will be held on October 4–6, 2018 in Moscow, Russia.

There are always future opportunities, but we must make them happen. Such opportunities usually come from our efforts. Ongoing engagement is the key. When we choose to disengage, we stagnate. Then either retirement or dementia is just around the corner. We must choose to keep our minds fully alive. Without our memories and our problem-solving abilities, we will be unable to remain resilient clinicians. Resilience, regardless of age, is a matter of engagement of the mind and the body. Once again, the choice is ours.

TEACHING VERSUS RELATING

Recent clinical findings suggest that it is not the technique that is effective, but rather it is the psychotherapeutic relationship that a clinician has with a patient that makes the difference (Ardito & Rabellino, 2011). Early in the senior author's career, I watched a colleague talk about duck hunting with a patient and observed that patient leaving feeling better. Where were the techniques that I had so carefully learned in graduate school? I am not suggesting that treatment techniques are not important. Rather, I am suggesting that, without developing a meaningful relationship with a patient, it will be very difficult, if not impossible, to teach that person self-acceptance and/or self-care. Furthermore, without having a good relationship with oneself, it is unlikely that a clinician will have the resiliency and empathy to help others. As Elizabeth Kübler-Ross, M.D. (1997), points out, this is about listening and caring. Specifically, patients feel relieved when they can share their "feelings with someone who cared" (p. 204). In a personal communication with Dr. Kübler-Ross many years ago, she spoke of her favorite research project at the University of Chicago Billings Hospital. The results showed that the most effective therapist was the person who listened and cared.

It seems that the belief that *knowing* (e.g., techniques and strategies) is superior to *being* is a common thought process, especially among young clinicians. Kottler (1993) points out, however, that *what we do* is not nearly as important as *who we are*. This is not meant to undermine the importance of excellent training; yet, as Kottler so beautifully states,

> It is not what the therapist does that is important—whether she interprets, reflects, confronts, or role plays—but rather who she is. A therapist who is vibrant, inspirational, charismatic; who is sincere, loving, and nurturing; who is wise, confident, and self-disciplined will have a dramatic impact through the sheer force and power of her essence, regardless of her theoretical alliances. (p. 3)

We would hypothesize, therefore, that the development of one's self—one's inner life, thoughts, feelings, and resiliency—is just as important, if not more so, than the development of one's knowledge and understanding. This is not a novel concept. The importance of *knowing thyself* has been proclaimed since the time of the ancient Greeks and is just as relevant today.

The issue is that many clinicians think that their personal lives and professional lives are separate. Whereas this viewpoint has some advantages, it also has several disadvantages. The *integrity* of a clinician is paramount. Integrity is often defined as "being honest and fair," but it is also defined as "the state of being complete or whole" (Integrity, n.d.). One cannot be whole *and* be divided. While there are a number of aspects in which personal and professional lives must remain divided, consistency of character must be a priority for clinicians in the helping professions.

Why is integrity important? We draw upon the energy that radiates from one another. Though try as we may, we cannot truly hide what is happening on the inside. As Wicks (2007) questions,

> ... What do people experience when they are with us? Do they experience a sense of respectful space where they can rest their burdens, anger, questions, projections, stress, anxiety, and wonder? Or, do they feel our sense of exhaustion, need to always be right or in control, or even our desire to be viewed as wise, attractive, witty, or helpful? What do people feel when they are with us... is an important question that we must reflect upon during the sessions and the times between them for the sake of ourselves as well as those we serve. (p. 5)

Wicks highlights the need for us to challenge our long-held schemas and reexamine our views of what it means to be clinicians.

RESILIENCE EXEMPLIFIED

Dr. Susanne M. Jensen is the epitome of an elegantly refined woman. Her presentation exudes perfection. Her suits are carefully pressed, her accessories are thoughtfully chosen, her makeup is on point (but not overdone), and her speech is precise (and laced with a beautiful German accent). Her demeanor and her very presence command attention, but not in a demanding fashion. When Dr. Jensen walks into a room, you *check yourself.* You stand a little taller, listen a little more intently, and speak a little more decisively. At the same time, you find yourself soothed, calmed, and inspired after just a few moments with her.

One may find it difficult to believe that Dr. Jensen, the American Group Psychotherapy Association's 2003 Woman of the Year; recipient of the 2013 Louisiana Group Psychotherapy Society's Lifetime Achievement Award; and recipient of the Louisiana Psychological Associations's (LPA's) 2016 Distinguished Psychologist Award (http://www.legis.la.gov/Legis/ ViewDocument.aspx?d = 1010341) was raised in war-torn Germany. In fact, during a recent dinner in which there were discussions of the pleasantries of childhood, Dr. Jensen revealed that, because of World War II, she did not have a childhood. Rather, it was all about surviving.

Despite many early traumatic experiences, Dr. Jensen persevered to become an incredibly influential clinical psychologist by profession and psychotherapist by vocation, as she described herself. In 1963, she earned a PhD from the University of Bonn in Germany and subsequently came to the United States on a Fulbright Fellowship. In addition to directing the Student Mental Health Services at Louisiana State University, Dr. Jensen also served as a member of the Louisiana State Board of Examiners of Psychologists, president of the Louisiana Group Psychotherapy Society, and United States Vice President of the World Council for Psychotherapy. Dr. Jensen has not only survived, but she has also thrived.

Recently, the LPA was pleased to invite Dr. Jensen to speak as a part of a symposium on resiliency in the practice of psychology (Nemeth, Matthews, Jensen, Shwery, & Bouillion, 2015). Dr. Jensen spoke of several lessons she learned throughout her lifetime that have helped her in developing a greater sense of resiliency. With Dr. Jensen's permission, the following discussion has been outlined and adapted from her 2015 speech.

Being Relational

Dr. Jensen explained that "being relational affirms my identity, meaning that even if I feel 'down', diminished, [or] injured in some way, being relational in my clinical work is an important factor contributing to my resilience" (para. 4). For the resilient clinician, being relational must also extend beyond clinical work. In discussing the occupational hazards of clinical work, renowned psychotherapist Irvin Yalom, MD (2002), examines the paradox of intimacy, stating,

> Yes, of course, the therapist's workaday one-to-one sessions are drenched in intimacy, but it is a form of intimacy insufficient to support the therapist's life, an intimacy that does not provide the nourishment and renewal that emanate from deep, loving relationships with friends and family. It is one thing to be

for the other, but quite another thing to be in relationships that are equally for oneself and the other. (pp. 251–252)

As clinicians, we must carefully cultivate our own personal relationships. We must tend to our own garden before cultivating the gardens of others. Yalom points out that, "At the end of our workday, having given so much of ourselves, we feel drained of desire for more relationship" and he warns that "we therapists run the risk of becoming less appreciative of family members and friends, who fail to recognize our omniscience and excellence in all things" (2002, p. 252). Therefore, we must guard ourselves against the temptation to withdraw from intimacy with family and friends, or to inadvertently disregard the important people in our lives.

Learning and Teaching

A love for both learning and teaching is another important factor of resilience. This is accomplished not just in the traditional classroom, but also via the *classroom of life*. As Dr. Jensen described, "Professional learning, learning from travels, learning from the lives of others is a joy. Believing that there is something new around the corner, to be curious, [and] to make discoveries" are crucial elements in developing a greater understanding of personal resilience (para 4).

Active Participation in Recovery

Dr. Jensen discusses the importance of actively participating in one's own recovery from illness. This applies to both medical and psychological forms of illness. We live in a "pill-popping" society. The Internet and television are riddled with advertisements by pharmaceutical companies, hailing the efficacy of the latest and greatest pill. Somehow, as a society, we have relinquished responsibility for our own health and well-being. Too many passively accept the consequences of poor lifestyle choices and daily decisions. Instead, the development of resilience requires ongoing, active participation in recovery. As Cloud (2010) states, "There is hope for people who…take ownership of where they need to grow" (p. 126).

Asking for and Receiving Help

As previously discussed, it is common for clinicians to primarily focus on the needs of others. In fact, genuine empathy is one of the characteristics that separate *good* clinicians from *great* clinicians. Dr. Jensen noted that, at one point, she "developed the grandiose notion, even the delusion, that others needed help but not me" (para. 4). It is imperative that we learn to ask for help and graciously allow ourselves to receive assistance.

A Life of Balance

Dr. Jensen describes balance as a fundamental "underpinning of resilience" (2015, para. 4). Extremism causes problems. This applies to work as much as to any other concept. For purpose-driven individuals, especially clinicians, learning to rest and to play can be quite difficult. This could be due to perceptions of rest and play as activities that are meaningless and lazy. We believe, however, that rest and play actually serve quite an important function! Rest and play are *active* processes that allow us to recharge and reenergize ourselves. When we learn to see these activities as essential processes in developing resilience and maintaining a healthy lifestyle, it becomes easier to make them priorities.

Looking Forward

There are many spices in the kitchen of life. One of them is having things to which you can look forward. Although it is obviously fun to look forward to big events, such as a vacation planned well in advance, a wedding, a birthday party, etc., we must develop a habit of looking forward to things on a daily basis. As Ruben (2007) describes, looking forward to things not only elevates our mood, but it can also promote growth by focusing on a bright future. These are not new concepts for clinicians. Practice today by taking time to plan and look forward to your next meal, a serene drive home from work, a bubble bath at the end of the day, or some quality time outside on the swing with your little one. Even seemingly mundane tasks, such as unpacking boxes after a big move, can become pleasant tasks when you work to cultivate a positive mindset.

Avoiding Cognitive and Relational Toxins

Dr. Jensen states that "sustained exposure to a threatening environment will lead to a breakdown in the form of some sort of violence or paralysis" (2015, para. 4).

If clinicians perceive therapy for their patients as a normal thing to do to process life's painful events, they must also perceive this as applying to themselves. The old saying, what is good for the goose, is also good for the gander, must apply. We are painfully aware of clinicians who are in need of treatment, but who will not seek it. Perhaps this is an example of false pride. Whatever the reason, this is problematic.

Also problematic is the belief that it is better to walk away from relationships rather than to fix them. We continue to be amazed at how many clinicians have been divorced two, three, or more times or have dysfunctional relationships with their children. How can you teach what you do not live? Perfect relationships are not required for they are impossible to achieve. But relationships based on mutual respect, empathy, and understanding are possible. Holding grudges, being disappointed in one another, and/or trying to control the relationship dynamics are coping strategies that do not work. They do not work in therapy either. Remember, even with children, the basis for a healthy relationship, whether personal or professional, is mutual respect.

THE BOTTOM LINE

We believe that it is helpful to allow oneself to learn from one's own experiences and the experiences of others when developing personal resilience. Nonetheless, we also believe that much of what makes an individual resilient can be narrowed down to two key concepts: a positive outlook and the ability to see oneself in tomorrow.

THE POWER OF POSITIVITY

Cognitive-behavioral therapy, arguably one of the most widely used psychotherapeutic approaches, is grounded in the relationship between thoughts, feelings, and behavior. Today, few people question the powerful connection between the mind and the body. Integrative medicine is at the forefront of many healthcare fields. On a day-to-day basis, however, consistently monitoring the health of one's thoughts is quite challenging. Perhaps this is why therapists are still in business; yet, this is challenging even for therapists!

As previously discussed, *what you know* matters far less than *who you are*. As clinicians, we must carefully and regularly examine the quality of our thought lives and subject ourselves, as Yalom (2002) says, to the "arduous, never-ending self-scrutiny and inner work required by our profession" (p. 256). As I (second author) tell my patients, the mind is like a garden. Of course, genetic predispositions and personality factors play a role, but we are still in charge of what we allow to grow in our garden. We must cultivate and maintain our garden on a regular basis.

What is growing in your garden? Are you planting beautiful flowers (e.g., love, joy, peace, future-directed thoughts) or is your garden overgrown with weeds (e.g., anger, hate, distress, negative thoughts)? Research has demonstrated time and time again the power of positivity, yet why do we struggle with this?

We believe that positivity can be cultivated. What you feed will grow. This implies an active, as opposed to a passive, process. We must actively seek out positive experiences, cultivate a positive, realistic mindset, and be aware of the power of negativity. As ancient Scriptures state, "We make a horse go wherever we want it to go by a small bit in its mouth. We turn its whole body by this. Sailing ships are driven by strong winds. But a small rudder turns a large ship whatever way the man at the wheel wants the ship to go" (James 3:3—4).

"The Sun Will Come Out Tomorrow"

As we previously mentioned, the hallmark of resilient people is their ability to be grounded in today, benefit from yesterday, and see themselves in tomorrow. The development of personal resilience is grounded in the ability to see oneself in tomorrow; and the ability to do this effectively is intimately linked to a positive, realistic mindset.

The film *Annie* is a wonderful story of overcoming personal obstacles. Annie's hallmark, of course, is being able to see herself in tomorrow, despite the challenges of today. As the song states,

The sun will come out tomorrow
Bet your bottom dollar that tomorrow
There'll be sun
Just thinkin' about tomorrow
Clears away the cobwebs and the sorrow
'til there's none
When I'm stuck with a day that's grey and lonely
I just stick up my chin and grin and say, oh
The sun will come out tomorrow
So you gotta hang on
'til tomorrow, come what may!
Tomorrow, tomorrow, I love ya, tomorrow
You're only a day away! (Strouse & Charnin, 1977)

IN SUMMARY

Resilient clinicians

1. Are firmly grounded in today. They
    a. Recognize, label, and share/resolve their feelings.
    b. Take care of their internal and external selves.
    c. Take care of their relationships, both personal and professional.
    d. Maintain good ethical boundaries.
    e. Seek therapy when needed.
2. They benefit from yesterday by
    a. Using memories to create balance.
    b. Maintaining perspective.
    c. Resolving past issues.
    d. Making wise choices.
3. They see themselves in tomorrow by
    a. Creating/planning stimulating experiences.
    b. Engaging in ongoing activities.
    c. Continuing to learn and grow.
    d. Staying related.
    e. Choosing to keep their minds and bodies fully alive.

In the final analysis, resilient clinicians know how to pace themselves, to maintain perspective, and to foster healthy relationships in order to care for themselves and others.

REFERENCES

Adler, R. F., & Benbunan-Fich, R. (2012). Juggling on a high wire: Multitasking effects on performance. *International Journal of Human-Computer Studies, 70*(2), 156−168.

Ardito, R. B., & Rabellino, D. (2011). Therapeutic alliance and outcome of psychotherapy: Historical excursus, measurements, and prospects for research. *Frontiers in Psychology, 2,* 1−11.

Bar-Levav, R. (1988). *Thinking in the shadow of feelings: A new understanding of the hidden forces that shape individuals and societies.* New York: Simon & Schuster.

Cloud, H. (2010). *Necessary endings: The employees, business, and relationships that all of us have to give up in order to move forward.* New York: Harper Collins Publishers.

Integrity (n.d.). *Merriam-Webster Online.* In Merriam-Webster. <http://www.merriam-webster.com/dictionary/integrity>. Accessed 15.01.17.

Kottler, J. A. (1993). *On being a therapist.* San Francisco, CA: John Wiley & Sons, Inc.

Kübler-Ross, E. (1997). *On death and dying.* New York: Scribner Classics.

Kushlev, K., Proulx, J., & Dunn, E.W. (2016). Silence your phones: Smartphone notifications increase inattention and hyperactivity symptoms. In *Proceedings of the 2016 CHI conference on human factors in computing systems* (pp. 1011−1020).

Muller, W. (1999). *Sabbath: Finding rest, renewal, and delight in our busy lives.* New York: Bantam Books.

Nemeth, D. G., Matthews, J. R., Jensen, S. M., Shwery, E., & Bouillion, K. (2015). Resiliency in the practice of psychology. In *Symposium presented at the Annual Convention of the Louisiana Psychological Association*.

Ruben, G. (2007). A key to happiness: having something to look forward to. <http://gretchenrubin.com/happiness_project/2007/08/a-key-to-happ-2/>. Accessed 2017.

Strouse, C. & Charnin, M. (1977). Tomorrow. Charles Strouse Publishing. <http://www.metrolyrics.com/tomorrow-lyrics-annie.html>. Accessed 15.01.17.

Wicks, R. J. (2007). *The resilient clinician*. New York: Oxford University Press.

Yalom, I. D. (2002). *The gift of therapy: An open letter to a new generation of therapists and their patients*. New York: Harper Collins Publishers.

CHAPTER 8

Promoting Resilience and Fostering Hope

Abstract

This chapter emphasizes the interconnection of resilience and hope as a state of the mind and a trait of the heart.

The text includes the definitions of, and differences between, joy and happiness.

The terms rational sequence (logical, goal-oriented) and ideological sequence (reactive) are explained in relation to the goal of the development of children into self-sufficient, productive, balanced, and resilient adults.

The authors emphasize that the management of anxiety, and identification and diffusion of anger, are skills that can be learned in order to develop emotionally.

A section describing the six domains of self-esteem illustrates crucial aspects of the development of resilience through emotional balance. The four stages of anger are presented in a table defining each stage along with intervention goals.

Keywords: Anxiety and anger management; comfort vs. distress; self-esteem; hope; joy

Contents

Innovative Approaches to Individual and Community Resilience
DOI: http://dx.doi.org/10.1016/B978-0-12-803851-2.00008-8

In Chapter 6, Achieving and Maintaining Individual Resilience, we described a teenager who was sexually victimized during the Age of Intimacy (Hendrix's sixth stage) and experienced years of traumatic distress and dysfunction. After eight emotionally painful years, this young woman finally made a choice to survive and thrive. She entered the RILEE Age of Choice—the Seventh Stage added by Nemeth, Ray, and Schexnayder (2003). As the authors stated, "When you create joy, maintain a balanced emotional state, and generate productive thoughts and behaviors consistently over time, then you have chosen the RILEE path" (p. 36). That is what this young woman did. Via therapy, she chose to resolve her emotional trauma and move forward. She chose freedom. She chose to complete a bachelor's degree, develop a healthy intimate relationship, and set goals for the future. She chose hope.

Hope is an integral component of resilience. This young woman made a decision to believe in herself, which is precisely how Lopez and his colleagues define hope (Lopez, Rose, Robinson, Marques, & Pais-Ribeiro, 2009). This young woman is no longer thwarted or controlled by her trauma; she is in the process of becoming.

Snyder and colleagues have written extensively on the concept of *hope* and how its strength manifests in our daily lives. The authors describe a recipe for hope that involve three simple ingredients: setting clear goals that reflect meaning and your personal values; developing a plan to achieve your goals; and sustaining your motivation to persevere (Nemeth & Whittington, 2012; Snyder et al., 2000).

In spite of her years of traumatic distress, this young woman chose to rebuild herself. Yes, she struggled. Yes, she had setbacks, even a hospitalization, but she kept on. Eventually, she regained her hope, her self-esteem, and her self-worth. Via therapy, these were gifts she gave to herself. Although they were torn from her in adolescence, although the struggle took years, she chose to overcome.

IT ALL STARTS IN CHILDHOOD

Resilience and hope are intertwined. Both are planted in early childhood. According to Snyder, Lopez, Shorey, Rand, & Feldman (2003), some may be classified as "higher hope" children and others are likely to be "lower hope" children (p. 124). Higher hope children are resilient, flexible, and adaptive. They are emotionally, psychologically, and socially well-balanced. According to Snyder, Hoza et al., these competent children are optimistic, whereas lower hope children are quite pessimistic. The latter children are prone to develop performance anxiety, self-doubt, ruminative thinking, and depression (Snyder et al., 1997, as cited in Snyder et al., 2003).

Higher hope children are creative, scholarly, and excellent problem-solvers. They tend to feel satisfied and appropriately satiated, whereas lower hope children tend to be unsatisfied and unsatiated. Nothing pleases them. There is no joy. Yet, joy does not fall from the sky. It is created. It is a gift that we choose to give ourselves.

JOY VERSUS HAPPINESS

Timothy Showalter, in a February 17, 2017 interview with Steve Inskeep of National Public Radio (NPR), stated that "to live a joyful life is different than living a happy life." This rather tough-looking singer/songwriter from Goshen, Indiana, apparently understood the difference. As Showalter stated, "Happiness is fleeting. Happiness is something that you're always going to reach for but you're never gonna quite get or be satisfied with." Instead, Showalter defined joy as "being fully engaged in life, whether it goes well or badly" (Inskeep, 2017).

That is what resilient people do. "The thrill of victory and the agony of defeat" as they used to say on the Wide World of Sports TV Program (1978), is what joy is all about. Full engagement no matter what the outcome! When children are allowed to go for the gusto, so to speak, they learn that the process is just as important as the outcome. Sometimes, the journey might even be more important.

HOPE CAN BE FOSTERED

Lopez, Boukwamp, Edwards, and Teramoto Pedrotti (2000) developed a classroom intervention program for elementary, middle, and/or high school students called "Making Hope Happen." Their findings reveal that hope can be fostered. Even those who have been victimized and/or traumatized, or who have observed such abuse, can learn to be hopeful.

According to Snyder et al., all students, even those with lower hope and those with fewer skills, can benefit from these group-based school programs (Snyder et al., 2003). These students' progress was measured by either the Children's Hope Scale for younger children or the Hope Scale for age 15 and above. In the program, their values, interests, and abilities were tapped; and their well-defined, nonabstract, goals were set.

Children then learned "stepping." They learned to develop "pathways of thinking" (Snyder et al., 2003), to develop sequences or smaller goals that are required to reach their ultimate goals. They also learned to develop "Plan B" or alternative pathways, just in case they hit a road-block. Children learned "stretch" goals as well (p. 130), which were defined as goals that simultaneously provided challenge and motivation. As it is evident from this research, children can learn to make healthy choices.

Teaching students to keep a diary of their ongoing self-talk is also quite important, especially for lower hope children who have been condi-tioned to negative self-talk. "I'm not important," "I can't succeed," and "I don't matter" are common themes for these children. These messages must be neutralized. Most children, according to Snyder and colleagues, are surprised to re-read their diaries and to see how poisonous their self-talk really is.

We recommend neutralizing these destructive messages by inviting children to "flip the thought" and to think the exact opposite of their negative thought. So "I am going to fail this test" then becomes "I am going to ace this test." Or "nobody will like my speech" becomes "every-body will love my speech;" or "I am ugly" is changed to "I am beautiful."

One of the first responses we often hear from children is, "But that's not true." We then remind the children that their negative thought is also not true, and we invite them to choose the more comforting, less distres-sing thought.

COMFORT VERSUS DISTRESS

According to Bowlby (1969), comfort and distress are our two earliest affective experiences. Nemeth et al. (2003) hypothesize that all other feel-ings are learned during the Six Developmental Stages described by Hendrix (1992, 1989). When things go wrong during these stages, chil-dren introject very negative messages and learn very maladaptive ways of thinking and dysfunctional ways of behaving. Therefore, lower hope stu-dents are at a higher risk of dropping out of school.

According to a May 12, 2012 story in the *Times-Picayune*, reporter Cindy Chang described Louisiana as "the world's prison capital."

She reported that Louisiana's incarceration rate is almost twice that of the national average with little opportunity for education and/or training. As Ms. Chang highlighted, "every dollar spent on prisons is a dollar not spent on schools, hospitals, and highways." In 2012, there were approximately 40,000 inmates in Louisiana prisons at a cost of $182 million a year. As Buck Foster, a former Professor at the University of Louisiana-Lafayette and an expert on Louisiana prisons, noted, "You have people who are invested in maintaining the present system" (Chang, 2012). Lastly, although elementary school reading scores reportedly do not predict future inmate populations (Graves, 2010), "one in three Louisiana prisoners reads below a fifth grade level" (Chang, 2012). So what chance do they have for rehabilitation? They have little hope and no resilience. They are doomed; most of them remain in prison until they die.

If we do not wish our children to end up in jail, we must foster resiliency skills and hopeful thinking as early as possible. Currently, Louisiana has the highest per capita incarceration rate of any state in the United States (Chang, 2012). This must change. Not only can we not financially afford this level of incarceration, but—more important—we also cannot emotionally or socially afford this pathway for our youth. As a society, we are failing our children. Education needs to include skill building and positive thinking. It needs to help our children to develop positive memories to sustain them on their lives' journeys. It needs to be about creating joy. All children, regardless of their home environment, must be taught to create joy. They must learn to (1) Believe in themselves, (2) Think wholesome thoughts, (3) Focus on positive feelings, and (4) Choose healthy behaviors. Children must also learn to process their choices in a responsive, rather than reactive, manner.

TEACHING SEQUENCES

Birnbaum (2013, Table 8.1) identifies two types of sequences: The Rational Sequence and the Ideological Sequence.

Table 8.1 Birnbaum's rational and ideological sequences

Rationale	Ideology
Ready	Ready
Aim	**Fire**
Fire	Aim

Too many people are using ideology rather than logical thought to guide their behaviors. These reactions, rather than responsive, contemplative choices, are creating havoc all over the world. Children must be taught logical, careful, goal-oriented sequencing.

THE GOAL OF CHILD DEVELOPMENT

The goal of child development, whether at home, at school, or in the community, must be to help children learn to be self-sufficient, caring, productive adults who contribute to their families and their communities and who understand the balance between work, family, and play (Nemeth et al., 2003). Basically, the goal of healthy child development is to produce resilient adults. As former First Lady Jacqueline Kennedy said in the early 1960s, "If you bungle raising your children, I don't think whatever else you do will matter very much" (*The Mini Page*, 2017).

MANAGING ANXIETY AND ANGER

In order to promote resilience, children must learn to manage anxiety and anger. If they do not learn how to develop these major skills of emotional development, they will become quite ideologically reactive. They will behave impulsively and create a path of destruction wherever they go. Anxious children may not be able to identify exactly what they are feeling, but they sense discomfort. As they have not learned to recognize, label, and share their feelings with others, they simply react in pain. They *bungle* it. After they have reacted, they may feel relieved, but ashamed. Angry children, however, can usually identify what they are feeling. After they react, they feel powerful, but lost. Their peers no longer want to be friends with them or connect to them. These children need to learn how to be powerful in wise ways. They need to learn to *relate*.

Children must learn to identify, label, and share their anxiety. Basic information, such as defining anxiety, explaining the various ways anxiety can present, and knowing what to do about it, is very important. We have found the work of Gary Emery, PhD, very helpful in this regard.

ANXIETY MANAGEMENT

One of our "go to" programs for anxiety self-management *is Overcoming Anxiety*, by Emery (1987). We have come to rely on Dr. Emery's clear and effective approach to help people understand and cope with anxiety. This audio series has served us well in our practice over the years. Although many more recent approaches are available, we continue to rely on this efficacious program.

Emery defines anxiety as "An emotional reaction to a distorted and unrealistic appraisal of a situation." He also points out that "Thinking creates anxiety [and] ideas about anxiety make it even more frightful" (1987).

He then notes that anxious symptoms may be fourfold: "Thinking, Emotional, Behavioral, and/or Physiological" (1987). Many people, especially children, have a very limited understanding of how anxiety can manifest physiologically. Most unknowing adults think that they are having a heart attack. This is unlikely, however, as many of these adults have been medically cleared by their physician and referred for anxiety management. Yet, never say never!

To examine the myriad of ways that anxiety can present, patients are invited to complete a Self-Esteem Inventory. As low self-esteem is correlated with lower hope and significant levels of anxiety and/or depression, this is very useful. Some of the symptoms that may be present include, but are not limited to, the following: Confused; Unable to direct thinking; Difficulty concentarting; Edgy; Tense; Anxious; Avoidant; Restlessness; Hyperventilation; Palpitations; Shortness of breath; Nausea. Many people, for example, do not understand that anxiety is a mood state. Thus, according to Emery, "What you think about and how you view the world will depend on your current mood. When you're in an anxious mood, your mind often wants to stay in that mood. With a drop in mood comes a drop in awareness. Focus creates energy. Thus, when you try to control your anxiety, you get more of it" (1987).

Emery then describes appropriate and inappropriate anxiety. For example, "Fear is appropriate if a real danger, which you are unable to handle, is present. Most of the time, when you are in a state of fear, you maximize the danger and minimize your ability to handle it" (1987).

The roots of anxiety and distorted thinking are then outlined as follows: "Your fear comes from some unknown source. When thinking is distorted, anxiety symptoms and motivation becomes activated. Many of your beliefs you developed as a child. You developed your self-image early in life. Your need to protect your ego or self-image reveals itself in the need for approval, the need for control, and the need to feel competent. Your needs, for approval, control, and competence, are powerful sources of anxiety" (1987).

These are usually the three intertwined components of anxiety; therefore, the needs for Approval, Control, and Competence must all be assessed. The next step is to explore which of these needs represents your "Achilles Heel," so to speak. Dr. Emery then offers the following cognitive approaches to correct anxiety distractions.

    a) The way to decrease your anxiety is to allow yourself to feel anxious
    b) Attempts to avoid anxiety keep it alive
    c) Emotions are signals to yourself from your brain telling you how to adapt to your environment. When you accept the signal the brain stops sending it.
    d) The trick is to accept the anxiety and stay in the situation.
    e) Anxiety is simply a signal to yourself and is no more dangerous than Morse code (1987).

This is followed by inviting people to accept, rather than resist, their anxiety.

ACCEPTANCE

Dr. Emery refers to the following as his "Awake Strategy," which has five specific components.

1. **Accept the anxiety.** Webster defines accepting as "giving consent to receive." Welcome it. Say "hello" out loud to yourself when it appears. Say, "I'll gladly accept this." Decide to be with the experience. Don't fight it. Replace your rejection, anger, and hatred of it with acceptance. By resisting, you're prolonging the unpleasantness of it. Instead, flow with it. Don't make it responsible for how you think, feel, and act.

2. **Watch your anxiety.** Look at it without judgement—not good, not bad. Don't look at it as an unwelcomed guest. Instead, rate it on a 0–10 scale and watch it go up and down. Be detached. Remember, you're not your anxiety. The more you can separate yourself from the experience, the more you can just watch it. Look at your thoughts, feelings, and actions as if you're a friendly, but not overly concerned, bystander. Dissociate your basic self from the anxiety. In short, be in the anxiety state, but not of it.

3. **Act as if you aren't anxious.** Normalize the situation. Act with the anxiety. Function with it. Slow down if you have to, but keep going. Breathe slowly and normally. If you run from the situation your anxiety will go down, but your fear will go up. If you stay, both your anxiety and your fear will go down.

4. **Keep repeating the first three steps.** Continue to 1) Accept your anxiety, 2) watch it, and 3) act as if you aren't anxious until it goes down to a comfortable level. It will, if you continue to accept, watch, and act with it. Just keep repeating these three steps: accept, watch, and act as if you aren't anxious.

5. ***Expect the best***. *What you fear the most rarely happens. However, don't be surprised the next time you have anxiety. Instead, surprise yourself with how you handle it. As long as you're alive, you will have some anxiety"* *(1987).*

The following ideas are offered by Emery to "catch distorted thoughts" and restructure thinking:

1. *Tell yourself you are going to "catch" your thinking*
2. *Own your own experiences*
3. *Approach what you fear*
4. *When you shudder, catch the images and thoughts that cause the shudder.*
5. *Experience fully the feelings you are trying to shut off.*
6. *Identify your inconsistences*
7. *Reward yourself when you catch a thought*
8. *Track your fears until you get back to the original fear.*
9. *Try to establish the significance of the event.*
10. *Slow your mind down.*

Emery then describes why facing what you fear is so important in overcoming anxiety. He outlines the following:

1. *When you avoid what you fear you experience anxiety.*
2. *Avoidance energizes fear because it keeps you from finding things out*
3. *You learn to deal with your anxiety when you are able to face it.*
4. *You generally use three avoidance mechanisms:*
   a. *You leave the frightening situation.*
   b. *You seek out assurance by continually reappraising the degree of threat.*
   c. *You respond by freezing.*

Emery points out that "the overall strategy is to do the opposite of what you are doing to avoid your anxiety" (1987). This is consistent with our "flip the thought" strategy.

Lastly, Emery encourages people to think behaviorally and learn Self-Trust.

SELF-TRUST = SELF ESTEEM

Self-trust is a matter of perception. In fact, Dillon & Benson (2001) define self-esteem as "the combination of how you perceive yourself and the value you place on the multi-dimensional self you see" (p. 10). It is composed of three parts:

1. What we *believe* about ourselves?
2. How we *feel* about ourselves?
3. How we *behave* or treat ourselves?

Self-esteem is also a gift we give ourselves. It is a choice. There are six domains of self-esteem or self-worth (Dillon & Benson, 2001). Throughout their book, *The Woman's Guide to Total Self-Esteem*, they emphasize that the following, which apply equally to men and women, are crucial aspects of developing self-esteem:

1. Relating to others in positive ways.
2. Expressing your personality through positive means.
3. Recognizing and understanding how you are appreciated by others.
4. Recognizing your intelligence and creativity.
5. Focusing on the good you do in the world.
6. Examining the ways in which you pursue what matters most to you in life.

These aspects of self-esteem require the development of the following good habits: self-acceptance (*as is*); being nonjudgmental; and being pro-self. Most important, these habits promote resilience. Resilience can be fostered by "crisis proofing" oneself. According to Dillon and Benson (2001), it consists of the following (pp. 144–145):

1. Seeking balance in all ways.
2. Focusing on the interactive body/mind/spirit connection.
3. Taking care of others starts with taking care of yourself first.
4. Staying in the present—remember the past is gone and the future is yet to be.
5. Treating yourself with loving kindness.
6. Remaining hopeful.

RESILIENCE AND EMOTIONAL BALANCE

One of the most important aspects of resilience is emotional balance, which is defined by Dillon and Benson (2001) as "the ability to restore calm when you are upset, get going when you are in a slump, and retain a capacity to think even in the face of intense emotions" (p. 84). Recognizing, labeling, and sharing your feelings allows you to monitor and self-regulate your feelings, before—not after—you lose control. Dillon and Benson (2001) recommend "being in charge of your feelings, rather than having your feelings be in charge of you" (p. 84). They conclude that "anger is often a disguise worn by more vulnerable feelings such as sadness, hurt, and fear" (p. 85).

In the next section we will discuss Anger Management. Dillon and Benson (2001), however, recommend that self-soothing strategies are a must! These strategies include, but are not limited to, the following: Containing, Releasing, Voicing, Relaxing, Stretching, Walking, Breathing, and Rocking (pp. 90—97). All are designed to increase comfort and reduce distress.

ANGER MANAGEMENT

Nemeth et al. believe that "healthy emotional expression involves sharing your feelings without deliberately hurting yourself or someone else. In a healthy RILEE family, sharing real feelings in a respectful way can lead to resolution. Resolution creates joy, even if that resolution is difficult. Having things resolved provides amazing relief and offers an opportunity to become closer" (Nemeth et al., 2003, p. 47). The key here is that resolution involves taking responsibility for your actions and having others pay attention to your concerns without intimidation. This can lead to empathy.

Empathy, or "being able to recognize and understand others' viewpoints," can be learned. But it must be practiced (Nemeth et al., 2003, p. 49).

Without empathy, people tend to be at war with their world. They are unable to interact rationally. They react with an ideological view that creates misery. They do not care about the effect of their behavior on others. Power and control are the desired results. The cost is irrelevant.

In a civilized society, however, the cost is relevant. Therefore, children must learn to sense, feel, and think before choosing an action (Nemeth et al., 2003, p. 58). In this manner, they can remain mindfully in the present while at the same time planning forward movement. Those who have experienced arrested development may react as they did in the past. They may become mired in that old affective theme and find themselves unable to move forward. Like a broken record, angry people, who are developmentally arrested, do not move forward. They just keep reacting the same way over and over again. They are stuck in the past. They are not free.

IGNITING ANGER

Murphy and Oberlin (2001), define four stages of anger (Table 8.2). If the experience is not processed and resolved in the present, similar events are likely to occur in the future.

For **Prevention**, Murphy and Oberlin suggest that adults do the following: address the child's immediate needs, avoid unnecessary frustration,

Table 8.2 Murphy and Oberlin's four stages of anger

Stage	Dynamic	Intervention goal
The Build Up	The past	Prevention
The Spark	The event	Diffusion
The Explosion	The reaction	Containment
The Aftermath	The result	Resolution

talk calmly, teach problem-solving skills, and understand the child's developmental level.

For **Diffusion**, the following are suggested: finding the true source of the problem, remaining calm, being a good listener, matching the face and the feelings, clarifying the rules, and offering diversion.

For **Containment**, a cooling off period is useful as are staying calm, separating entanglements, avoiding threats and bargaining, and restating disciplinary agreements.

For **Resolution**, talking things out is essential as are teaching better problem-solving skills, managing outbursts before they escalate, having regular family meetings, and being consistent with discipline (Nemeth et al., 2003).

Although these ideas were written for anger management with children, most can also apply to adult interactions.

As we reviewed the various signs of anxiety earlier in this chapter, we will now identify the warning signs of anger. According to Nemeth et al. (2003), physiological warning signs include a flushing face, sweating, feeling hot, staring intensely, tightening lips, stiffening body, avoiding eye contact, squinting eyes, looking disgusted, and breathing shallowly. These warning signs are all a part of the **Build Up**. When people start exhibiting any of these "red alert" signs, so to speak, they are moving toward an **Explosion**. Then, the slightest comment can **Spark** or ignite their anger.

But why choose anger? Perhaps it is a defense or a stopper, or a weapon to make a child or an adult *feel*. In the end, however, it damages relationships and the **Aftermath** can have serious consequences.

10 DEFENSIVE TRAITS

According to Murphy and Oberlin (2001, as cited in Nemeth et al., 2003), angry children have 10 major defensive traits:

1. They make their own misery.
2. They cannot analyze problems.

3. They blame others for their misfortune.
4. They turn bad feelings into mad feelings.
5. They lack empathy.
6. They attack people rather than solve problems.
7. They use anger to gain power.
8. They indulge in destructive self-talk.
9. They confuse anger with self-esteem.
10. They can be nice when they want to be.

ANGRY CHILDREN BECOME ANGRY ADULTS

Without early intervention, angry children become angry adults. As they haven't learned to recognize, label, or share their more vulnerable feelings and/or needs, their anger tends to surface instead. Therefore, nothing gets resolved. Without early and/or adult intervention, they become and remain developmentally arrested in Hendrix's Stage 2. These adults typically have toxic relationships, which do not last. As they do not know how to connect, these angry adults keep making the same mistakes over and over again. They are not resilient.

CHANGE CAN HAPPEN

Yes, change can happen; but it takes courage and a desire to change life-long angry traits. Nemeth et al. (2003) suggest changing angry traits to RILEE traits by substituting

1. Joy for misery
2. Clarity for confusion
3. Responsibility for blaming
4. Good feelings for bad feelings
5. Empathy for disdain
6. Positive choices for defensive choices
7. Relatedness for control
8. Constructive self-talk for destructive self-talk
9. Mastery for power
10. Kindness for manipulation

KINDNESS CAN HELP

Robin L. Flanigan espouses "The Kindness Cure" (2017). She points out that "self-criticism is only going to keep you stuck—especially if it's fueling depression and anxiety. Replacing disapproval and judgement with self-compassion allows you to accept your flaws, real or perceived, in a way that strengthens mental wellness" (p. 29). It also strengthens resilience. Kristin Neff, PhD, is cited by Flanigan for her research on self-compassion. Neff "breaks self-compassion into three dimensions: self-kindness, common humanity, and mindfulness" (p. 30). She points out that there is a societal misconception about self-kindness, suggesting that it is either self-indulgent or narcissist. We agree with the author that this misperception must be changed. Self-kindness, which one of our women's therapy groups labeled as "pro-self," is an important ingredient in being able to establish and maintain Intimacy (Hendrix Stage 6; 1998, 1992).

Why be harsh when you can be kind? Introjecting negative messages from parents and/or society in general is so damaging. These externally based messages are bad enough, so why add internal ones to them? In this way, we destroy hope.

FOSTERING HOPE

Instead of destroying hope with either externally or internally based negative self-talk, we must contain these messages and create hope. "Hope matters," as Lopez succinctly stated in his 2010 lecture to the Louisiana Psychological Association's members. In quoting President John Fitzgerald Kennedy, Lopez noted, "We must think and act not only for the moment, but for our time" (Lopez, 2010).

Our time is now and resiliency is needed to sustain it and create a meaningful future. We must be high-hope people, who, as Lopez defined, are "people who believe that the future will be better than the present and... have the power to make it so." He quoted Snyder's definition of hope as "a life-sustaining force that is rooted in our relationship with the future" (Lopez, 2010). So, how do we foster hope? Just as Antoine de Saint-Exupery did—by teaching people "to long for the endless immensity" (Cottmeyer, 2016) of the future... a future that is filled with possibilities. As Lopez stated, there is such "excitement that comes from pursuing your goals, discovering and using your strengths, and collaborating with others" (Lopez, 2010). Having hope makes you feel like you matter.

How does this happen? As Showalter (2017) states, by enjoying the journey. With positive self-messages, laughter, faith, and love, hope does spring eternal. But, Lopez (2010) notes that you must:

1. *Define* it for yourself.
2. *Find* it wherever you can.
3. *Encourage* hopeful bonding to others.
4. *Create* ways of exchanging hope and
5. *Remind* yourself daily of the benefits of being hopeful.

PROMOTING RESILIENCE

To summarize, hope must be clearly defined. It can be both a trait of the heart and a state of the mind. It flourishes in healthy relationships. It can be crystalized to form good memories. Daily reflections, mini-interventions, reconnections, and clear definitions of goals and objectives all combine to nourish both the heart and the mind. This is how we promote resilience.

REFERENCES

Birnbaum, R. (2013). Ready, fire, aim: The college campus gun fight. *Change, 45*(5), 6–14, Philadelphia, PA: Taylor & Francis Group.

Bowlby, J. (1969). *Attachment and loss.* New York: Basic Books.

Chang, C. (2012). Louisiana is the world's prison capital. *The Times Picayune.* Retrieved February 20, 2017, from <http://www.nola.com/crime/index.ssf/2012/05/louisiana_is_the_worlds_prison.html>.

Cottmeyer, M. (2016, January 05). Longing for the endless immensity of the sea. Retrieved March 10, 2017, from <https://www.leadingagile.com/2016/01/longing-for-the-endless-immensity-of-the-sea/>.

Dillon, S., & Benson, C. (2001). *The woman's guide to total self-esteem: The eight secrets you need to know.* Oakland, CA: New Harbinger Pub.

Emery, G. (1987). *Overcoming anxiety* [CD]. BMA Audio.

First lady, first mom. (2017, February 19). *The Mini Page.* Issue 07.

Flanigan, R. L. (2017, February 4). The Kindness Cure: Challenging your inner critic with a little self-love can have radical results. *Esperanza.*

Graves, B. (2010, March 23). Prisons don't use reading scores to predict future inmate populations. *The Oregonian.* Retrieved February 20, 2017, from <http://www.oregonlive.com/education/index.ssf/2010/03/prisons_dont_use_reading_score.html>.

Hendrix, H. (1989). *Getting the love you want: A guide for couples.* New York: Institute for Relationship Therapy.

Hendrix, H. (1992). *Keeping the love you find: A guide for singles.* New York: Simon and Schuster, Inc.

Inskeep, S. (2017). *When reality is more intense than psychedelics: Strand of oaks on 'hard love'* [Interview]. Baton Rouge, LA: 89.3 WRKF.

Lopez, S. J., Boukwamp, J., Edwards, L. E., & Teramoto Pedrotti, J. (2000). *Making hope happen via brief interventions. Presented at the 2nd positive psychology summit in Washington, DC.*

Lopez, S. J., Rose, S., Robinson, C., Marques, S. C., & Pais-Ribeiro, J. (2009). Measuring and promoting hope in schoolchildren. In R. Gilman, E. S. Huebner, & M. Furlong (Eds.), *Promoting wellness in children and youth: Handbook of positive psychology in the schools* (pp. 37−51). Mahwah, NJ: Lawrence Erlbaum.

Lopez, S. L. (2010). Hope: It's more than a feeling. *Presented at the 62nd annual convention of the Louisiana Psychological Association in Baton Rouge, LA.*

Murphy, T., & Oberlin, L. H. (2001). *The angry child: Regaining control when your child is out of control.* New York: Clarkson Potter Publishers.

Nemeth, D. G., Ray, K. P., & Schexnayder, M. M. (2003). *Helping your angry child.* Oakland, CA: New Harbinger.

Nemeth, D. G., & Whittington, L. T. (2012). Our robust people: Resilience the face of environmental trauma. In D. Nemeth, R. Hamilton, & J. Kuriansky (Eds.), *Living in an environmentally traumatized world: Healing ourselves and our planet* (p. 133). Santa Barbara, CA: ABC-Clio/Praeger.

Snyder, C. R., Hoza, B., Pelham, W. E., Rapoff, M., Ware, L., Danovsky, M., et al. (1997). The development and validation of the Children's Hope Scale. *Journal of Pediatric Psychology, 22,* 399−421.

Snyder, C. R., Lopez, S. J., Shorey, H. S., Rand, K. L., & Feldman, D. B. (2003). Hope theory, measurements, and applications to school psychology. *School Psychology Quarterly, 18*(2), 122−139. Available from <http://dx.doi.org/10.1521/scpq.18.2.122.21854/>.

Snyder, C. R., Tran, T., Schroeder, L. L., Pulvers, K. M., Adams, V., & Laub, L. (2000). Teaching the hope recipe: Setting goals, finding pathways to those goals and getting motivated. *Summer, Reaching Today's Youth,* 46−50.

CHAPTER 9

Teaching Resilience

Abstract

This chapter defines the biological, psychological, and social aspects of resilience. Exposure, social support, and coping and loss of resources are topics included in discussing these three aspects of resilience. Positive, supportive, and hopeful family interactions are shown to be vital in recovery from traumatic events.

The phenomenon of the ripple effect, that is, transitioning from helpfulness and empathy to exhaustion and resentment, is explored. The definitions of the terms empathy and sympathy are compared and contrasted. Sample of strategies for teaching and cultivating resilience, available on an individual level, or in a workshop experience are highlighted.

As in previous chapters, spirituality is shown to play a role in restoring traumatized individuals to a more hopeful, resilient state.

Keywords: Biopsychosocial; meaning-making vs sense-making; posttraumatic stress disorder; cornerstones

Contents

Resilience is a biopsychosocial phenomenon (Rodin, 2014). Many are fortunate to have a biological propensity to be resilient. Some are not so fortunate. According to the research of Genomind, Inc. (2016), a company specializing in personalized medicine through genetic testing, some individuals are more prone to develop stress reactions and/or posttraumatic stress disorder (PTSD), as well as other adverse effects, than those whose *CYP450* and *SLC6A4* genes can process selective serotonin

Innovative Approaches to Individual and Community Resilience
DOI: http://dx.doi.org/10.1016/B978-0-12-803851-2.00009-X

reuptake inhibitors and other psychotropic medications normally (Samer, Ing Lorenzini, Rollason, Daali, & Desmeules, 2013; Xie et al., 2006; Xie, Kranzler, Farrer, & Gelernter, 2012).

Biology is, however, only one of three aspects of resilience. The other two (i.e., psychological and social factors) are of equal importance. This chapter will focus on these psychosocial aspects of resilience. As we have been focusing on the resilience of Louisiana's environment and its people, the readers are referred to Editor Katie E. Cherry's book on *Lifespan Perspectives on Natural Disaster, Coping with Katrina, Rita, and Other Storms* (2009) for a review of the literature in this regard. Some of the more salient aspects of Dr. Cherry's book are, however, reviewed below.

RESEARCH MATTERS

Dr. Cherry and her colleagues address the long-term negative consequences of such storms on children, adolescents, adults, and families. She highlights Nelson's work on "the protective factors that promote survival, recovery, and resilience in the face of a natural disaster" (2008, pp. 57–69). These researchers share reactions to significant stressors on a continuum from acute stress disorder to PTSD.

Jones et al. (2009) focus on the following factors: *Exposure* (the strongest predictor of PTSD symptoms), *Social Support* (a major protective factor), *Coping* (either active or avoidant), *Resource Loss, Ethnicity, Age and Gender*, and *Parent–Child Interaction*. As their results regarding Ethnicity and Age and Gender were somewhat equivocal, these factors will not be discussed below.

Exposure: This is conceptualized on two dimensions: (1) the number of stressors and the relative severity of each stressor (Norris & Elrod, 2006) and (2) the fearful thought of self or others death or physical proximity to disaster (Cherry, 2009). In this regard, exposure was found to be the strongest predictor of PTSD symptoms and emotional dysregulation.

Social Support: This term was defined in Jones et al.'s (2009) chapter as "social interactions or relationships that provide individuals with actual assistance or that embed individuals within a social system believed to provide love, care, or senses of attachment to a valued social group or dyad" (p. 76). They cite the work of Hubfoll and Stokes (1988) in this regard, concluding that, as a protective factor, higher levels of social support tended to decrease PTSD symptoms. Thus, social support can actually moderate the relationship between exposure and PTSD symptoms.

Social support by social services and mental health professionals can actually serve as a buffer to mitigate the effects of stress.

Coping: Jones et al. (2009) cite the definition of coping by Folkman, Lazarus, Gruen, and DeLongis (1986) as follows: "Coping can be defined as cognitive and behavioral efforts to manage environmental and internal demands that are appraised as taxing or exceeding personal resources" (p. 77). Coping has two factors: *Active* (seeking social support and problem-solving, which can prevent PTSD) or *Avoidant* (avoiding emotions and social withdrawal, which can lead to PTSD). Active coping strategies contribute to resilience. Jones et al. conclude, however, that "the severity of the trauma overwhelms the child's ability to cope" (p. 78).

Resource Loss: Jones et al. (2009) rely on Freedy, Shaw, Jarrell, and Masters (1992) definition, "as the loss of personal and social resources which results in diminished coping capacity and psychological distress" (p. 78). These include objects (home), conditions (employment), personal characteristic (skills), and energies (money). They conclude that "the driving mechanism behind the psychological distress following a trauma is loss of resources" (p. 78) and that it is a major predictor of PTSD.

Parent—Child Interaction: Parents' levels of distress have a significant effect on the level of distress of the child(ren).

Jones et al. (2009) then cite Masten's 2006 *Resilience Model*. Masten defines *resilience* as "positive patterns of functioning during or following an adversity" (p. 84). They point out, however, that "the resilience structure has neglected to include mental health outcomes in the conceptualization of resilience" (p. 84).

The research of Mancini and Bonanno (2006) defines *resiliency* as "an individual quality or set of qualities which prevent a person from developing psychopathology following a traumatic event" (Davis, Tarcza, & Munson, 2009, p. 100). The following qualities that lead to resilience were cited as: self-enhancement, repressive coping (i.e., avoiding the grief), "hardiness, positive emotion and laughter, optimism, and access to prompt intervention following a disaster" (p. 100). Bonanno, Galea, Bucciarelli, and Vlahov (2007) also outline several demographics that are associated with greater resiliency, such as male gender, having less than a college education, not losing income after a disaster, and increased social support. Benight and Bandura (2004) identify "coping self-efficacy" as believing that one has the capacity to handle trauma, which leads to greater resilience (as cited in Davis et al., 2009, p. 160). This tends to "mediate the relationship between exposure to a traumatic event and acute and long-term distress following the event" (as cited in Davis et al., 2009, p. 101). Prayer can also help (McLeish & Del Ben, 2008). Displacement, however, does not help, nor does previous psychopathology (McFarlane, 1989).

FAMILY MATTERS

The old adage "every cloud has a silver lining," may be apropos here. There are some *meaning-making* benefits that have been found to emerge postenvironmental trauma. According to Davis, Nolen-Hoeksema, and Larson (1998), these benefits are threefold: "Improved relationships, prioritization and planning, and reappraisal" (as cited in Garrison & Sasser, 2009, p. 113.) Also four *sense-making* themes emerge: "order in social environment, attribution to a higher power, general acceptance, and old adages survive" (p. 113). The use of humor is also helpful. Therefore, in conclusion, Garrison and Sasser describe that "[making] people a priority, [and understanding that] weather happens, hope rules, and humor helps" (p. 113), are all things that can encourage family resilience.

Families are one of the most important social entities. They have strength. They can find meaning even in the worst of circumstances (Davis et al., 1998). Garrison and Sasser define a resilient family as one that "remains hopeful, focuses on how their strengths can help them through the situation, adopts a 'can do' attitude, and accepts the aspects of the situation that are out of their control" (p. 114). With spirituality and transcendence, Walsh (2003) concludes that families find a way to work through adversity.

This process was quite apparent in the aftermath of Louisiana's Great Flood of 2016. The matriarchs of a family to whom we spoke noted that all of their four daughters and sons-in-law came immediately to help them cope with the 3 inches of water in their ancestral home, even though some had over 18 inches to 3 feet of water in their own homes. They rallied around each other, embraced the challenges, took one another in (i.e., provided shelter to the three who had flooded), and thanked God that they all had survived.

Six months post-trauma, most have now returned or are nearly ready to return and move back into their homes. The family described above clearly had an experience in changing their perspective and in understanding what really mattered. Instead of conflict, there was an alignment of goals. They also gained an enhanced appreciation for one another.

They were able to experience the flood as a "wake-up call," which resulted in a reappraisal of the success of their survival efforts (Garrison and Sasser, 2009, p. 119). They survived and thrived. They maintained order by framing the event logically (e.g., "What do you expect, we live in South Louisiana!"). They relied on their faith in God to carry on. They accepted the situation, and they used old adages to help them cope. This optimistic family also used humor in their interactions (e.g., "Out with the old and in with the new. We intended to remodel anyway."). Humor can absolutely facilitate healing (Berk & Tau, 1989; Ruxton, 1988). Garrison and Sasser offer the following keys to resilient coping:

1. *Make People and Pets a Priority.* We learned this from Hurricane Katrina. Pets are a part of the family. For example, during the Great Flood of 2016, one man gallantly rescued a drowning woman from a sinking car only to be asked to go back for her pet (Kunzelman, 2016). He did so at his own peril and she was forever grateful. The car was not important. The fluffy white dog was!

2. *Weather Happens.* If you live in Louisiana and/or any place near water, you must expect problematic weather conditions (e.g., hurricanes, tornados, floods) from time to time. "That's the price of living in paradise," as many Louisianans would say. The key is to be prepared.

3. *Hope Rules and Humor Helps.* Another key to resilient coping is to maintain hope. As Lopez (2011) notes, we must pursue our own goals, discover and use our strengths, and collaborate with others. That is what this South Louisiana family did to survive and thrive. The matriarch of the family, just 6 weeks post-knee-replacement surgery, said "We're better than ever."

Garrison and Sasser (2009), however, did offer these cautions:

1. "One size doesn't fit all"—be aware of the cultural components when planning interventions (Knowles et al., 2009).

2. "Life doesn't just stop because you've perceived a disaster" as was apparent from the matriarch's post-flood knee-replacement surgery.

3. "Do no harm" (Knowles et al., 2009).

4. "Don't underestimate the sapping ability of heat and humidity," especially in places like South Louisiana.

5. "Ripple effects are greater than the storm surge" (i.e., the effects on the helpers, rescuers, and those who take in the evacuees) (Cherry, 2009).

BEWARE OF RIPPLE EFFECTS

In Baton Rouge this "ripple effect" was no more apparent than in the days, weeks, and months following Hurricane Katrina. Once a sleepy college town/state capital of approximately 300,000 people went from helping "those Katrina people" to loathing them. The first author's daughter was to marry in Baton Rouge 3 months post-Katrina. All of the hotels that had been booked for this rather large wedding had been commandeered by Governor Kathleen Blanco for the "Katrina people." Over 100 out-of-town wedding guests had to stay with in-town wedding guests who graciously offered to help. Bed-and-breakfast (B & B) hideaways in remote places had to quickly be called into service as well (most B & B owners were still reeling from their Red Cross guests). Many guests wanted to come to bear witness not only to the wedding ceremony, but also to tour the devastated parts of New Orleans, which they did. It was indeed an awkward time. But the wedding was not canceled. The couple's honeymoon, however, had to be rebooked from the Maya Rivera in Mexico, that was hit by Hurricane Wilma, to a sister resort in Cabo San Lucas, that was not at all happy about being required to pick up the overflow. Just like the Katrina people in Baton Rouge, the Maya Rivera honeymooners who were displaced to Cabo felt like a burden on that sister resort. So, on all levels, taking in displace people can be difficult for all parties involved.

ATTITUDES MATTER

In order to teach resilience, it is necessary to understand not only the culture of the people, but also the attitude that these individuals possess. In Dr. Akiko Mikamo's (2013) memoir, *Rising from the Ashes: A True Story of Survival and Forgiveness from Hiroshima*, she emphasizes the importance of attitude. She acknowledges her parents, Shiya and Miyoko Mikamo, "for having the strengths and resilience to survive the atomic bomb, rebuilding their lives, from nothing, and bringing my sisters and me into the world. They taught me the importance of forgiveness and having empathy for others, especially for those who have different backgrounds, beliefs and, values" (p. ix).

In spite of the pain and suffering they endured because of the August 6, 1945 bombing, the Mikamos found a way to survive and thrive. Their path was forged on attitude and hard work. At one point, Mr. Mikamo told his daughter, Akiko,

It's wrong to hate Americans. Yes, they bombed us, but the Americans are not to blame. You have to see the bigger picture of what was happening in the world at that time. It's the war to be blamed. I want you to grow up, learn English and learn about other cultures, and become a bridge across oceans to help people learn from different backgrounds, with different beliefs understand one another, so no one will ever suffer from a nuclear bombing again. Contribute to society and contribute to world peace (p. 168).

That is exactly what Akiko Mikamo, Psy.D., M.P., has done. As she stated, "My father taught me, once again, how we as human beings have a choice to react to seemingly negative experiences with compassion and forgiveness. I could choose to foster feelings of anger and resentment or I could choose to be grateful..." (p. 168). This comment was in response to her father's only surviving possession, her grandfather's pocket watch, having been stolen when it was on display at Hiroshima Exhibit at the United Nations. Mr. Mikamo pointed out that, "the pocket watch was merely a belonging" (p. 169), not the essence of their family's history. He added, "The pocket watch was just an object, its symbolism and meaning were created by us, it did not intrinsically carry them" (p. 169).

Since that conversation, Dr. Akiko Mikamo has striven to understand the difference between sympathy and empathy. She learned that,

"Sympathy is when you feel the same or similar emotions with the person you feel sympathy for," whereas *"empathy is different. You can empathize with people without feeling the same feelings or agreeing with their views...Empathy is when you put aside your own subjective experiences and see things from the other person's perspective, considering their upbringing, culture, and personality to understand how that person might feel, think, and see"* (p. 170).

As Dr. Mikamo stated, "My father chose to empathize with the Americans, to understand the context and environment they were in that led to the dropping of the atomic bomb. He chose to use this experience as an opportunity to better understand human behavior, rather than to remain a victim to lifelong chains of anger, judgement, and detachment" (pp. 170–171). Dr. Akiko Mikamo, who is now a clinical and medical psychologist in San Diego, CA, and the first author's dear friend, certainly lives by this philosophy.

CHOICE MATTERS

We have previously discussed the choice that one young adult female survivor of childhood sexual abuse made. After years of difficulty she chose to survive and thrive. But it was not easy. Bogar and Hulse-Killacky (2006) summarize "*5 determinant clusters* (interpersonally skilled, competent, high self-regard, spiritual, and helpful life circumstances) and *4 process clusters* (coping strategies, refocusing and moving on, active healing, and achieving closure)" (p. 318). They cite the work of Lev-Wiesel (2000), which concludes that perceptions were crucial to outcomes (Bogar & Hulse-Killacky, 2006). Specifically, Lev-Wiesel reported that "survivors who attributed the abuse to the offenders characteristics reported a higher quality of life and were better able to maintain fairly intact self-esteem than were individuals who assumed all blame or blamed situational factors for the abuse" (p. 318). As is apparent, choice matters.

TO TEACH OR NOT TO TEACH

One cannot teach what one does not understand! Fortunately or not, 90% of the people in the world have experienced some sort of trauma in their lives (Rehm, 2015). Therefore, most people are experientially equipped to either teach and/or learn more about resilience. Teaching about resilience, however, does require perspective. An understanding of the biopsychosocial aspects of resilience is crucial as is an appreciation for the current research on the type of resilience being taught (i.e., resilience in the aftermath of environmental trauma, sexual trauma, violence, death/loss). In this chapter, resilience in the aftermath of environmental trauma and sexual trauma has been emphasized. The importance of family and culture, attitudes, beliefs, and philosophy and the cognitive, affective and behavioral choices that one makes matter. All of the above are integral components of teaching resilience. One should not intervene without understanding these factors.

Regardless of good intentions, "do no harm" (Knowles et al., 2009) is still the Golden Rule. For example, in the aftermath of Hurricane Katrina, well-meaning Red Cross volunteers from throughout the country came to help (Nemeth, Hamilton, & Kuriansky, 2012), but they did not understand the culture. Many mistakes were made. People were separated from their families, pets were not allowed to evacuate with their owners, religious organizations were not allowed to provide culturally appropriate meals to evacuees in the Louisiana State University Maravich Basketball Arena, diabetics were served honey buns for breakfast at the Southern University A.W. Mumford Field House, local psychologists with Red Cross training were turned away, etc. All in all, the Red Cross interventions were a disaster. During Louisiana's Great Flood of 2016, local people took charge. The "Cajun Navy" did not wait to be called. They acted immediately. Steve Wheeler of *The Advocate* recounted the heroism of these volunteers:

> During the flood, I witnessed incredible acts of bravery as the 'Cajun Navy' res-cued desperate people from the rising water; many of them friends in my neighborhood. The Cajun Navy, an unorganized group of private boat owners, assembles during the natural disasters not because they're paid, but because they care about helping others. Shortly after the flood, one local lawmaker blew his reelection chances when he proposed licensing and charging fees to boat owners who wanted to help their neighbors.
>
> While the Cajun Navy came to the rescue in the hours and days right after the flood, I also saw acts of...let's call it 'timidity.' I watched three military troop vehicles idle at the edge of a flooded road for two hours while stranded residents waited on the other side, darkness approaching.
>
> Later, after dark, two of Louisiana's 'Cajun Navy' pilots risked their lives shut-tling my neighbors across the moving water. I was in one of the boats when two of these brave airboat pilots rescued the final two neighbors from Victory Lane. It was about 10:30 p.m. in pitch black water full of who knows what (Wheeler, 2017, p. 2J).

As a result, only 13 people lost their lives as compared to thousands in Katrina. As Nemeth and Whittington (2012) stated, "Local people do this best" (p. 123). Therefore, we must remember that the local people are the experts, not out-of-town volunteers, government officials, the military, etc. For example, one of the most important priorities in the aftermath of Hurricane Katrina was bottled water. It was hot. People were thirsty. The humidity was high. The military brought bottled water in by helicopter, but dropped it instead of lowering it to the ground. The bottles broke. Chaos ensued. It took all of the efforts of Lieutenant General Russel Honorè to restore order (Nemeth & Kurianksy, 2015). Again, another example that local people do it best.

TO LEARN OR NOT TO LEARN

Learning begins early on in life. One's parent(s) or parent-figure(s) are the most important teachers in one's life. They guide infants, children, and adolescents through each developmental stage, as described in earlier chapters. Choices are made. On the parent's part, healthy choices must be taught and behaviorally demonstrated. On the child's part, these choices must be introjected and imitated. Choosing to be "a part of" rather than "a part from" one's family is crucial. Children must learn that is it important to be present, to see the world as a wonderful and exciting place, to develop an identity, to be successful, to belong, and to be close and loving (Hendrix, 1989, 1992). They must choose to learn these basic messages in their families. But not all children learn/accept these healthy messages, and not all parents are capable of teaching their children these healthy messages. Addiction, mental illness, social injustice, lack of availability, as well as many other variables, may prevent the transition of healthy developmental messages from parent to child.

Oftentimes, these children are sent off to school without being armed with these healthy messages. Schools are ill-equipped to teach such values. Children are left adrift, frequently absorbing unhealthy messages from their peer groups. They may be emotionally drained or too afraid to learn. As Mikamo (2013) stated, "Most aggression is a reaction to fear" (p. 171), and aggression may result from inadequate preparation for facing the world.

And then there is trauma, expected or unexpected. It happens to 90% of us (Rehm, 2015), so we must rise to the occasion to meet it. Meeting trauma with healthy developmental messages is *easier*, but certainly not easy, than meeting trauma with unfinished developmental issues.

Perhaps this is a starting point. Determining whether or not an individual has unfinished developmental issues is needed in order to teach trauma resilience. According to Murphy and Oberlin (2001), if individuals present as frantic, angry, troubled, defective, lonely, or indulgent, more so than is situationally appropriate, they may be stressed by not only the current situation (state), but also their longstanding adaptation to dealing with crisis (trait). As Bogar and Hulse-Killacky (2006) pointed out, they may not have the five determinant clusters and four process clusters in place to deal with the crisis they face. Finding out which of these factors may be lacking and teaching these skills may be very helpful. The operative word here is "teaching," not "rescuing." Doing it for them is not the same thing as doing it with them. Except in extreme situations of danger (e.g., being in a sinking car), most people want to learn how to cope and move forward. They want to learn to survive and thrive. They long to be resilient.

As individuals may have regressed to a previous and/or different developmental stage, it is important to remember what Knowles et al. (2009) concluded, "One size does not fill all." Therefore, interventions to teach resilience must be tailored to where the individual is rather than to where you would like that person to be. You must respond with empathy, not sympathy. This will allow you to choose appropriate interventions. Then, learning is possible.

A SMORGASBORD OF CHOICES

Teaching resilience requires having a smorgasbord of coping strategies available and choosing the ones that best fit the individual and the situation. Although an overall strategy is helpful (e.g., like the ones offered in our Emotional Resiliency Workshops), the specifics were tailored to the participants' needs. Information was provided, people were heard, group process and relaxation exercises were included, and attendees left with a myriad of resources.

These ideas included, but were not limited to, the following:
1. Accept support
2. Arrange to be heard
3. Set realistic goals
4. Plan the next step
5. Continue healthy habits
6. Learn from the past
7. Get adequate sleep and exercise
8. Schedule "self-time"
9. Continue family traditions
10. Share the burden
11. Be flexible
12. Maintain hope and humor.

LISTENING, UNDERSTANDING, AND RESPONDING

Most important, participants were encouraged to remember that thoughts lead to feelings and that feelings lead to actions. Choice was the key. Developing these 12 positive external and internal resources, as Rodin (2014) points out, is crucial to one's ability to survive and thrive posttrauma (see tables in Chapter 4, Community Resilience: Baton Rouge—A Community in Crisis—Grieving and Moving Forward).

In the first author's 2016 Keynote Address to the First World Congress on Mental Health in Moscow, Russia, Nemeth concluded, "We often hear, but do not listen. We often judge, but do not understand. We often act, but do not know why." Teaching resilience requires listening, understanding, and responding, not reacting. We must teach the art of listening attentively, not allowing ourselves to think ahead or prepare our response. We must understand with empathy and clarity, making sure that the other person's thoughts and feelings have truly been heard. We must respond with compassion and connection by reassessing our goals and objectives and making sure that they are in sync with the needs and values of the other person. This is not psychological first aid as described by Garrido (2007), but rather it is effective intervention to preclude victimization (Nemeth & Whittington, 2012). Nemeth and Whittington conclude, "Tragedy itself does not victimize people, rather, falling into a state of hopelessness, despair, and/or depression victimizes people" (pp. 114–115). Avoiding this negative result can be accomplished by teaching healthy coping strategies, the earlier the better. Resilience can be learned at home, at school, and in the community.

SPIRITUALITY MATTERS

As Zelinski (2012) notes, resilience may be found at "The Intersection of Nature, Psychology, and Spirituality." She adds that "the role of spirituality factors heavily into a shift from pathology to post-traumatic growth" (p. 169).

As in South Louisiana, "the influence of spirituality permeates not only the coping methods involved in achieving post-traumatic growth but also the relationship between people and their natural environment" (Zelinski, 2012, p. 176). She proposes the need "to explore the view of people as adaptable and resilient rather than disordered and dysfunctional in response to natural disasters" (p. 177).

TEACH THE CORNERSTONES

So, what must we teach? According to Dr. Gloria Alvernaz Mulcahy (2012), we must teach the cornerstones of resilience: Responsibility, Reciprocity, Respect, and Relationships, as the Oneida Haudenosaunee people do (Nemeth et al., 2012). We must also teach understanding, vigilance, history, citizenry, trauma resolution, proactive and prosocial behaviors, the inevitability of change, and the need for harmonious living (Nemeth et al., 2012). Native Americans have known these cornerstones for centuries. Perhaps we can learn and teach these resilient values as well.

REFERENCES

Alvernaz Mulcahy, G. (2012). Our indigenous people: Healing ourselves and mother earth. In D. G. Nemeth, R. B. Hamilton, & J. Kuriansky (Eds.), *Living in an environmentally traumatized world healing ourselves and our planet*. Santa Barbara, CA: Praeger/ABC-CLIO, LLC.

Benight, C. C., & Bandura, A. (2004). Social cognitive theory of posttraumatic recovery: The role of perceived self-efficacy. *Behaviour Research and Therapy*, *42*(10), 1129−1148. Available from http://dx.doi.org/10.1016/j.brat.2003.08.008.

Berk, L. S., & Tau, S. A. (1989). Neuroendocrine influences of mirthful laughter. *The American Journal of the Medical Sciences*, *298*(6), 390−396. Available from http://dx.doi.org/10.1097/00000441-198912000-00006.

Bogar, C. B., & Hulse-Killacky, D. (2006). Resiliency determinants and resiliency processes among female adult survivors of childhood sexual abuse. *Journal of Counseling & Development*, *84*(3), 318−327. Available from http://dx.doi.org/10.1002/j.1556-6678.2006.tb00411.x.

Bonanno, G. A., Galea, S., Bucciarelli, A., & Vlahov, D. (2007). What predicts psychological resilience after disaster? The role of demographics, resources, and life stress. *Journal of Consulting and Clinical Psychology*, *75*(5), 671−682. Available from http://dx.doi.org/10.1037/0022-006x.75.5.671.

Cherry, K. E. (2009). *Lifespan perspectives on natural disasters: Coping with Katrina, Rita, and other storms*. Dordrecht: Springer Verlag.

Davis, C. G., Nolen-Hoeksema, S., & Larson, J. (1998). Making sense of loss and benefiting from the experience: Two construals of meaning. *Journal of Personality and Social Psychology*, *75*(2), 561−574. Available from http://dx.doi.org/10.1037//0022-3514.75.2.561.

Davis, T. E., Tarcza, E. V., & Munson, M. S. (2009). The psychological impact of hurricanes and storms on adults. In K. E. Cherry (Ed.), *Lifespan perspectives on natural disasters coping with Katrina, Rita, and other storms*. New York, NY; Dordrecht: Springer Verlag.

Folkman, S., Lazarus, R. S., Gruen, R. J., & DeLongis, A. (1986). Appraisal, coping, health status, and psychological symptoms. *Journal of Personality and Social Psychology*, 571−579.

Freedy, J. R., Shaw, D. L., Jarrell, M. P., & Masters, C. R. (1992). Towards an understanding of the psychological impact of natural disasters: An application of the conservation resources stress model. *Journal of Traumatic Stress*, *5*(3), 441−454. Available from http://dx.doi.org/10.1007/bf00977238.

Garrido, G. (2007). Trauma resolution and lifestyle change. *Paper presented at the 60th annual United Nations DPI/NGO conference midday workshops*. New York.

Garrison, M. B., & Sasser, D. D. (2009). Families and disasters: Making meaning out of adversity. In K. E. Cherry (Ed.), *Lifespan perspectives on natural disasters coping with Katrina, Rita, and other storms*. New York, NY; Dordrecht: Springer Verlag.

Genomind, Inc. (2016). Literature summary—Genecept Assay 2.0. Retrieved from https://portal.genomind.com/Assets/Summaries/Summary_v2016-01.pdf.

Hendrix, H. (1989). *Getting the love you want: A guide for couples*. New York: Institute for Relationship Therapy.

Hendrix, H. (1992). *Keeping the love you find: A guide for singles.* New York: Simon and Schuster, Inc.

Hubfoll, S. E., & Stokes, J. P. (1988). The process and mechanics of social support. In S. Duck, D. F. Hay, S. E. Hubfoll, W. Ickes, & B. M. Montgomery (Eds.), *Handbook of personal relationships: Theory, research and interventions* (pp. 497–517). Oxford, England: John Wiley & Sons.

Jones, R. T., Burns, K. D., Immel, C. S., Moore, R. M., Shwartz-Goel, K., & Culpepper, B. (2009). The impact of hurricane Katrina on children and adolescents: Conceptual and methodological implications for assessment and intervention. In K. E. Cherry (Ed.), *Lifespan perspectives on natural disasters coping with Katrina, Rita, and other storms.* New York, NY; Dordrecht: Springer Verlag.

Knowles, R., Sasser, D. D., & Garrison, M. E. B. (2009). Family resilience and resiliency following hurricane Katrina. In R. P. Kilmer, V. Gil-Rivas, R. G. Tedeschi, & L. G. Calhoun (Eds.), *Meeting the needs of children, families, and communities post-disaster: Lessons learned from hurricane Katrina and its aftermath.* Washington, DC: American Psychological Association.

Kunzelman, M. (2016). Louisiana woman finally meets the man, her 'angel,' who saved her in dramatic flooding rescue. *The Advocate.* Retrieved from http://www.theadvocate.com/louisiana_flood_2016/article_9fc27752-79ae-11e6-94a0-6b9e9a6f4b90.html.

Lev-Wiesel, R. (2000). Quality of life in adult survivors of childhood sexual abuse who have undergone therapy. *Journal of Child Sexual Abuse, 9*(1), 1–13. Available from http://dx.doi.org/10.1300/j070v09n01_01.

Lopez, S.L. (2011). Hope: It's more than a feeling. *Presented at the 62nd annual convention of the Louisiana Psychological Association.* Baton Rouge, LA.

Mancini, A. D., & Bonanno, G. A. (2006). Resilience in the face of potential trauma: Clinical practices and illustrations. *Journal of Clinical Psychology, 62*(8), 971–985. Available from http://dx.doi.org/10.1002/jclp.20283.

Masten, A. S. (2006). Developmental psychopathology: Pathways to the future. *International Journal of Behavioral Development, 30*(1), 47–54. Available from http://dx.doi.org/10.1177/0165025406059974.

McFarlane, A. C. (1989). The aetiology of post-traumatic morbidity: Predisposing, precipitating and perpetuating factors. *The British Journal of Psychiatry, 154*(2), 221–228. Available from http://dx.doi.org/10.1192/bjp.154.2.221.

Mcleish, A. C., & Del Ben, K. S. (2008). Symptoms of depression and posttraumatic stress disorder in an outpatient population before and after Hurricane Katrina. *Depression and Anxiety, 25*(5), 416–421. Available from http://dx.doi.org/10.1002/da.20426.

Mikamo, A. (2013). *Rising from the ashes: A true story of survival and forgiveness from Hiroshima.* Lulu Publishing Services.

Murphy, T., & Oberlin, L. H. (2001). *The angry child: Regaining control when your child is out of control.* New York: Clarkson Potter Publishers.

Nelson, L. P. (2008). A resiliency profile of hurricane Katrina adolescents. *Canadian Journal of School Psychology, 23*, 57–69.

Nemeth, D., Hamilton, R., & Kuriansky, J. (2012). *Living in an environmentally traumatized world healing ourselves and our planet.* Santa Barbara, CA: Praeger/ABC-CLIO, LLC.

Nemeth, D. G., & Kuriansky, J. (2015). *Ecopsychology: advances from the intersection of psychology and environmental protection* (Vol. 2 Santa Barbara, CA: Praeger/ABC-CLIO, LLC.

Nemeth, D. G., & Whittington, L. T. (2012). Our robust people: Resilience the face of environmental trauma. In D. Nemeth, R. Hamilton, & J. Kuriansky (Eds.), *Living in an environmentally traumatized world: Healing ourselves and our planet* (p. 133). Santa Barbara, CA: ABC-CLIO/Praeger.

Norris, F., & Elrod, C. (2006). Psychosocial consequences of disaster: A review of past research. In Fran H. Norris, Sandro Galea, Matthew J. Friedman, & Patricia J. Watson (Eds.), *Methods for disaster mental health research* (pp. 20−44). New York, NY: Guilford Press.

Rehm, D. (2015). The science of resilience and how it can be learned [Audio blog post]. Retrieved February 13, 2017, from http://dianerehm.org/shows/2015-08-24/the-science-of-resilience-and-how-it-can-be-learned.

Rodin, J. (2014). *Being strong in a world where things go wrong: The resilience dividend*. New York, NY: Public Affairs Publishing.

Ruxton, J. P. (1988). Humor intervention deserves our attention. *Holistic Nursing Practice*, *2*(3), 54−62. Available from http://dx.doi.org/10.1097/00004650-198802030-00010.

Samer, C. F., Ing Lorenzini, K., Rollason, V., Daali, Y., & Desmeules, J. A. (2013). Applications of CYP450 testing in the clinical setting. *Molecular Diagnosis & Therapy*, *17*, 165−184. Available from http://dx.doi.org/10.1007/s40291-013-0028-5.

Walsh, F. (2003). Family resilience: Strengths forged through adversity. In F. Walsh (Ed.), *Normal family processes* (3rd ed., pp. 399−423). New York, NY: Guildford.

Wheeler, S. (2017). The Cajun Navy. *The Advocate*, p. 2J.

Xie, P., Kranzler, H. R., Farrer, L., & Gelernter, J. (2012). Serotonin transporter 5-HTTLPR genotype moderates the effects of childhood adversity on posttraumatic stress disorder risk: A replication study. *American Journal of Medical Genetics Part B: Neuropsychiatric Genetics*, *159B*(6), 644−652. Available from http://dx.doi.org/10.1002/ajmg.b.32068.

Xie, P., Kranzler, H. R., Poling, J., Stein, M. B., Anton, R. F., Brady, K., . . . Gelernter, J. (2006). Interactive effect of stressful life events and the serotonin transporter 5-HTTLPR genotype on posttraumatic stress disorder diagnosis in two independent populations. *Archives of General Psychiatry*, *66*(11), 1201−1209.

Zelinski, S. (2012). Our critical issues in coping with environmental changes: The intersection of nature, psychology, and spirituality. In D. G. Nemeth, R. B. Hamilton, & J. Kuriansky (Eds.), *Living in an environmentally traumatized world healing ourselves and our planet*. Santa Barbara, CA: ABC-CLIO.

CHAPTER 10

Conclusions

Abstract

This chapter reviews the study of resilience: how it is defined, how it is used, how it can be taught, and how it might be learned. The authors purport that resilient people are grounded in the present, have learned from the past, and are preparing for the future. Such individuals, including clinicians, are ordinary, everyday people, who know how to take care of themselves. They know how to survive and thrive. Healthy, engaged families and communities foster individual resilience and competence. They care for one another and their environment.

Keywords: Fostering resilience and competence; cherishing one another and the environment

Content

We have defined resilience as the ability to be firmly grounded in today, while benefitting from the yesterday so that we can imagine ourselves in tomorrow. It is about hope, connectedness, commitment, and perseverance. It can be taught. It can be learned. It can be cherished.

As 90% of the world's people have experienced some sort of trauma in their lifetime (Rehm, 2015), trauma has become a part of the life of "ordinary people." In fact, we do not know of anyone who has not been affected by adversity. Thus, we are all, in a sense, "ordinary people" just trying to survive and thrive.

It all begins with attachment, role modeling, and imitative learning. Learning healthy attachment, emotional regulation, self-awareness, and mastery are important developmental milestones for children. For healthy development, children need good role models—parents, teachers, advisors—and a caring community.

This process, to quote Dr. Ann Masten (2014), is about the "Ordinary Magic" of becoming resilient. Just like resilience, competence can be learned. The message, "I can" is so important. Armed with the tools of resilience and competence, anything is possible.

Innovative Approaches to Individual and Community Resilience
DOI: http://dx.doi.org/10.1016/B978-0-12-803851-2.00010-6

These healthy messages all begin in healthy families. Hendrix's work (1989, 1992) is used to explore and explain childhood development. His work is fresh and easy to understand. Murphy and Oberlin's work (2001) on the dynamics of unhealthy families allows many important comparisons.

Children then move from their families into various community settings (e.g., school, church, work). In such settings, they are often exposed to crises—from social upheaval to environmental trauma. When communities are struck by trauma (e.g., Hurricane Katrina or Louisiana's Great Flood of 2016), what happens? Usually, a six-stage psychological process takes over. It starts with Shock, then Survival Mode, Assessment of Basic Needs, Awareness of Loss, Susceptibility to Spin and Fraud, and Resolution (Nemeth & Whittington, 2012). This process may take a very short time or a very long time. For children, whose schools were inundated with water by the Great Flood of 2016, it seemed to take forever. Finally after 6 months, most schools were back in operation. The children watched their parents, their teachers, their churches, and their communities try to cope with this overwhelming event. They not only watched, but they were also deeply affected.

It was very hard, but people persevered. They helped one another. They overcame adversity. Psychologists, as well as other mental health professionals, helped to prepare adults and children for the forthcoming holidays. Via Emotional Resiliency Workshops, coping strategies were demonstrated.

And then there was the environment! Rebounding from the Great Flood of 2016 was not an easy task. As in Hurricane Katrina and in the tornadoes that followed a few months after the Great Flood of 2016, the environment began to absorb the shock, people began to rebuild, and life went on. Seemingly, it has been easier for the environment to recover from natural rather than human-caused disasters. In many respects, this can be said for people as well. The aftermath of floods, for example, appears to be easier, not easy, to deal with than the aftermath of abuse. Maintaining individual resilience is much harder post abuse.

In both situations, the role of the family is crucial. Children, even adult children, long for the protection of home—their "oikophilia"—their special place where everything will be okay. Like Dorothy in *The Wizard of Oz* said, "There's no place like home" (1938).

In spite of all of the environmental traumas that Louisiana experiences, over 80% of people born in Louisiana stay in Louisiana (Lane, 2014).

Perhaps it is the longing to be close to the family or the culture or the food. Whatever the reason, it is an almost unbreakable bond. When asked why Nemeth (the first author) stayed in Louisiana after obtaining her PhD from Louisiana State University, she tells people—"It's the 5 F's— family, food, friends, fun, and football! After all, where else is Mardi Gras an official two-day holiday! And, in Louisiana, football is more than a sport; it's a religion."

And then there is biology. Many are born with the biological propensity for resilience. Some are not. As resilience is considered to be a biopsychosocial phenomenon (Rodin, 2014), having this biological propensity makes life a little easier. In either case, the psychosocial aspects of resiliency can be overwhelming at times. People must learn to conquer their fears, cope with their needs, and choose healthy ways of moving forward so that they can recover and rebuild. In Louisiana, this is essential, for—it is not *if* there will be another hurricane or flood or tornado, it is *when*. We must be prepared!

So must psychologists, psychotherapists, social workers, and other mental health professionals who care for traumatized people be prepared. This is not easy, especially when you have also been traumatized. It is easier, however, when you yourself are a resilient clinician.

Resilient clinicians have usually experienced trauma themselves; however, it is what they have learned, how they have coped, and how they have ordered their lives that makes the difference. When resilient clinicians have their lives in order, they are better able to empathically care for others. They are firmly grounded in today, they have learned from yesterday, and they are prepared to cope with tomorrow. Thus, they can be fully present to help others. Being fully present requires daily self-care. These clinicians exemplify resilience. They are relational and balanced individuals who avoid toxic situations and look forward to the future with wonder and excitement. Yes, such people do exist and one is described in this book.

Resilient clinicians foster hope, for hope is the psychological basis of human existence. It helps us to get from *here* to *there*. It helps us to cope with adversity. It helps us to learn and grow. It creates a wisdom beyond our imagination. It moves us forward to the moon and beyond. It is the essence of truly living, not merely existing. In times of trauma, it helps us to make positive choices, to believe in tomorrow, and to cherish life itself. With hope, there is joy, not neccessarily happiness, and life is experienced with gusto, not fear, whatever the outcome. Anxiety and anger can dampen this process, but skills to manage these strong emotions can be learned. Remember, it is what we believe about ourselves, how we feel about ourselves, and how we behave or treat ourselves and others that really count. When we give ourselves the gifts of resilience, hope, and self-esteem, we are better prepared to face the challenges that lie ahead.

For those of us who are parents and/or teachers, we are in a unique position to help children learn to be resilient. First, by example. Displaying resilient skills is so important. Then, by understanding resilience. It is very difficult, if not impossible, to model or teach what we do not understand. We each have multiple experiences that have called upon us to be resilient. The more we learn about being resilient, the more effective teachers we can be.

In conclusion, this book has emphasized the importance of family and community life. Both are essential factors in shaping the resilience and in cherishing the resolve of "ordinary" people. Our "not so ordinary" future, however, is up to us.

REFERENCES

Hendrix, H. (1989). *Getting the love you want: A guide for couples.* New York: Institute for Relationship Therapy.

Hendrix, H. (1992). *Keeping the love you find: A guide for singles.* New York: Simon and Schuster, Inc.

Lane, E. (2014). Louisiana has most native-born residents in the country, New York Times reports. *The Times Picayune.* Retrieved from http://www.nola.com/.

Masten, A. (2014). *Ordinary magic: Resilience in development.* New York: The Guilford Press.

Murphy, T., & Oberlin, L. H. (2001). *The angry child: Regaining control when your child is out of control.* New York: Clarkson Potter Publishers.

Nemeth, D. G., & Whittington, L. T. (2012). Our robust people: Resilience the face of environmental trauma. In D. Nemeth, R. Hamilton, & J. Kuriansky (Eds.), *Living in an environmentally traumatized world: Healing ourselves and our planet* (pp. 113–140). Santa Barbara, CA: ABC-CLIO/Praeger.

Rehm, D. (2015). The science of resilience and how it can be learned [Audio blog post]. Retrieved February 13, 2017, from http://dianerehm.org/shows/2015-08-24/the-science-of-resilience-and-how-it-can-be-learned.

Rodin, J. (2014). *Being strong in a world where things go wrong: The resilience dividend.* New York, NY: Public Affairs Publishing.

The Wizard of Oz [Motion picture]. (1938). New York: MGM/UA.

EPILOGUE

Resilience is *the* requirement of our time. We must honor our past, revel in our present, and look forward to our future. We must be fully present, even at times when it is difficult or uncomfortable to do so. We must see what must be seen. We must know what must be known. We must do what must be done. We must resiliently face the requirements of living in our ever-changing world.

Nothing stays the same, even though we would like for our world, our families, and, perhaps, ourselves, to remain so. All things and all people evolve. As resilient people, we must prepare ourselves and our communities for change. Calculators are out. Computers are in. We must embrace change and evolve with it. Resistance is futile. Resilience is necessary.

With change, however, comes renewed traditions and values. Our longing for home, for our special place, our "oikophilia," for our people, etc., will always be there. What do we leave behind? What do we take with us? Happiness may not always accompany change, but joy can. Embracing necessary change is often quite a challenge, but one we can meet. That is what resilience is all about. We will find a way to adapt, we always do!

Darylne G. Nemeth and Traci W. Olivier

INDEX

Note: Page numbers followed by "*f*" and "*t*" refer to figures and tables, respectively.

Edwards Brothers Inc.
Ann Arbor MI. USA
February 21, 2018